Dear Dolly

Emily Lineberger Bridges

Edited By: **Susan Stafford, Canada**

Cover Design
& Inside Illustrations By: **Bonnie Shields, Sandpoint, Idaho**

Graphics By: **Kristen Spinning, Kromatiks, Tucson, Arizona**

Dear Dolly is available in tack stores, bookstores and can be ordered via the Internet by visiting, http://TheCompletePet.com. Retail price is $19.95 (U.S. funds).

K&B Products
P.O. Box 1502, PMB 214
Red Bluff, CA 96080
to inquiry@TheCompletePet.com on the Internet. Visit us on the Web
at http://TheCompletePet.com

ISBN#: 0-9646181-7-6

FOREWORD

Let me begin by saying that I am not attempting to write a how-to book but rather a *how not-to* book. I had virtually no practical experience with horses when I embarked on my horse keeping adventure. My love of horses paved the way and sheer determination followed. I made a lot of mistakes early on, but each one was a learning experience. Throughout the book I will mention some particular challenges and tips that worked for me.

The stories are real and those who know me would agree that I lack the imagination to fabricate the events. It is my hope that when you read of my trials and tribulations and see that a dream can be realized, you will take up the gauntlet and live your own horse dream.

People have asked me why I re-entered the world of horses with such frenzy. I did not want to miss out on another moment. I wasted a lot of years and it is important that I make up for that lost time. Granted, there is a lot of hard physical work involved, but I would much rather work hard and live out my horse dream than lift weights in a gym somewhere. I think of it as exercise without the boredom. And when you read the book you will see that life is certainly never boring at Summerwind Farm!

This book is written for those of you who love spending time with your horses or wish for horses of your own. Not everyone shows his or her horses. Some people just like being around them. I genuinely love to ride my horses and work with the foals, but I get tremendous satisfaction when I linger after feeding time to listen to the sounds of sweet feed and hay crunching. I love to groom the horses during evening rain showers and listen to the sound the rain makes on the tin roof amidst the horses' whinnies. And I am perfectly content to sleep in the tack room for the pleasure of hearing the night noises our horses make. This is why I have horses.

My husband, Ron, who had never seen a real horse before I became involved with them again, is my partner in this endeavor. In spite of his lack of experience with horses, Ron put his knowledge of construction to good use. With the help of his father, brother and brother-in-law, all of whom had little or no construction experience, he built a wonderful barn in which to house our equine family members. When my yearning for more horses became evident, he brought out the tools again and expanded the existing barn to accommodate our ever-growing family.

I am amazed by our progress in five years and look forward to the next five. This is my therapy and a dream come true. You too can "Live the Dream". If I can do it, anyone can!

Table Of Contents

Foreword 3

Dedication 5

Part One - The Awakening 7

Chapter 1   Dear Dolly 11

Chapter 2   A Dream Comes True 15

Chapter 3   Let The Games Begin 26

Chapter 4   Auja Maria, My Soulmate 40

Part Two - A New Beginning

Chapter 5   The Birth Of Summerwind Farm 44

Chapter 6   The Orientation 59

Chapter 7   Lilli's New Baby And A Mysterious Illness 69

Chapter 8   Shaikh, Joy And Sorrow 85

Chapter 9   The Barn Grows 92

Chapter 10   Whizteria, My Silver Lining 94

Part Three - Growing And Glowing

Chapter 11   Maria's Summer Miracle 100

Chapter 12   Trials And Tribulations 114

Chapter 13   A New Life Brings A Challenge 122

Chapter 14   Making A Change 129

Chapter 15   Life Goes On At Summerwind 138

Chapter 16   An Agonizing Decision 145

Chapter 17   The Breeding Season And A Place In Time 158

A Final Word 167

Part One
The Awakening

For most of my adult life, I had been involved with raising a family. My world was wrapped up in my two daughters, and although their father and I had divorced, I strived to keep his relationship with them intact. Through this difficult time, I left my childhood dreams in less-than-greener fields and horses became a part of my past. In fact, if someone asked me about my childhood on the farm, my reply would be, "I could hardly wait to get away from that kind of life."

I remarried, my children grew up and I divorced again. I found myself completely alone for the first time in my life. I began to throw myself into my career as a bank officer, working long hours arranging mortgage loans in Asheville, North Carolina. At that point in my life, nothing mattered more to me than being successful in business and being able to rely solely on myself. I had a great income from commissions earned while interest rates were at an all-time low. This, plus the fact that Asheville was a very desirable locale for retirees and those wishing to relocate from other more populated areas to the beautiful, serene mountains of Western North Carolina, made banking very lucrative. My business thrived. I had substantial savings, a beautiful old house in the city (far away from my rural upbringing), a BMW in the garage and I was totally, happily independent. I was very satisfied with my life.

Or so I thought. In 1992, the bank at which I worked enrolled me in a self-awareness weekend with a psychological behavioral group. I did not want to participate, especially after I learned that the group included executives from all walks of life, from all over the United States. However, I had no choice, because I was tactfully told that my management style was "too harsh", and I needed to find out why. Reluctantly, I packed and went to the retreat, not knowing what to expect.

The method used at this particular retreat was one in which psychologists take you through stages of your life that made an impact, whether conscious or subconscious, and have you face those times. In a quiet room with soft music playing, the entire group lay on the floor with their eyes closed. The facilitator told them to focus on a time when they were around twenty years of age and to accept the first image that came to mind. "This is ridiculous. I will not participate", I kept telling myself over and over. But when the time came to focus, I saw the wedding to my first husband. Well, I knew how that ended.

Next, the facilitator told the group to focus on something that happened when they were thirteen. Bingo! What I had not expected to see again happened. I saw the face of my beloved childhood horse, Dolly. It was an image that I had put out of my mind years ago. How strange that it now re-surfaced. Needless to say, the tears flowed. And, although there were other revelations during the weekend session that helped me see the need for a change in my management style, none had the same impact on me as seeing Dolly's face. I knew that I had to ride a horse again as soon as possible.

Immediately upon arriving back home in Asheville, I began to call riding stables. For some odd reason, my ex-husband, Ron, came to mind. He had moved to another city an hour and a half away, but we remained friendly and spoke occasionally by phone. He had never been around a horse in his life and I remember him once saying that he was afraid of them. Nevertheless, I decided that I wanted him to accompany me when I rode for the first time.

I called Ron and mentioned that I felt the need to go riding again. He suggested that I get in the riding mode by going to see the movie "Wyatt Earp", starring Kevin Costner. I could not fathom why a man with a military background and no horse sense would want to go see that movie, but I agreed to go to see the movie with him -- if he would go riding with me. I literally heard the sheer fright through the phone line, but this man who never denied me anything uttered a weak "Okay."

The movie was three hours long and we both felt as though we had been riding all day when it was over. But we were surely in the western mode. I called a local stable and arranged for us to take a two-hour ride the next morning. I was very excited. At least it was a start.

When we arrived, the man who was in charge of the trail ride matched us up with horses, I assume based on what he thought we looked like we needed. My ex had a decent mount and after instruction on how to use the reins, he managed to land on top of the horse. Now, it was my turn.

The white horse's name was Rosie and she looked to be about a hundred years old. She would not move in any direction. Obviously, Rosie was not my ideal choice of a mount after all these horseless years. The man told me to kick her and kick her I did. Still, unless all the other horses were moving, Rosie stood still. It was a very frustrating two hours. I was not discouraged, however.

The next weekend, I called a riding stable about thirty minutes from Asheville. This stable advertised guided rides through the Pisgah National Forest, which sounded like a lot of fun if I was better mounted this time. Early on Sunday morning, I arrived at the stable and was disappointed to find that only one other customer was there. I was afraid that they wouldn't take just the two of us out, but the guide admitted that she would really enjoy a nice, peaceful ride without having to worry about a group. This time, I was given a really nice horse named Barnaby, who, prior to coming to Asheville, had lived in the Virgin Islands. He did speak English very well and was good with leg commands, so we got along famously. The ride was very pleasant and I knew I had to do it again. It became a Sunday routine and I was a regular, at times even helping out with guiding on the trail.

Then I decided I wanted more. At this point in time, I was not ready to commit to uprooting my life, selling my home and buying another property where I could keep a horse. But I definitely needed something more than routine trail rides each week. That's when the stable owner mentioned to me that she would be willing to lease Barnaby for a year. He would be at my disposal any time I wanted to ride. The best part was that all of his upkeep would be taken care of by her employees. It was a good situation and I happily accepted.

Each weekend through the summer and on winter days when possible, I rode Barnaby. Guides at the stable who wanted to practice their trail riding skills usually accompanied me. Sometimes the owner of the stable packed a picnic lunch for us and we rode the trails for the entire day.

I had no fear of winter riding until a very snowy, icy Sunday morning found four of us deep in the forest. All of the horses were shod and the temperature had dipped to 0 degrees, with a wind chill factor of minus 30 degrees. The waterfalls were all frozen and the roads were sheets of ice.

Several horses fell as we slowly made our way down the trails. It suddenly occurred to me that we were indeed crazy!

For the first time I was a little nervous and even the stable owner, a seasoned professional rider, expressed hesitation at continuing. I was not going to throw in the towel, but much to my relief the owner insisted that we go back to the lodge and have some hot chocolate. I didn't try any heroics in that type of weather again. I felt a lot better taking the conservative route that didn't include riding a shod horse on icy roads and over frozen streams. I prayed for an early spring.

The riding went very well for the remainder of the winter and into spring. Barnaby was a very well-mannered horse and was always willing to take me for a pleasant ride in the forest. But with warmer weather, I began to seriously consider how great it would be to have my very own horse. I began to think of my dear Dolly more often. The next chapter will explain why.

♊♋

Chapter One
Dear Dolly

I grew up on a working farm in North Carolina, the youngest of three children. My brothers helped my father with the everyday operation of the farm and I helped my mother with the household chores. In my family, it would have been unheard of for a girl to do farm work, especially the work involving caring for and doctoring the horses we used for work first and then for pleasure. I wasn't allowed to watch breeding or birthing, but I could help with the grooming. That became my favorite pastime after my inside chores were completed to my mother's satisfaction.

When I was five years old, my father bought a special horse named Dolly that he assigned to me for grooming. She was a fifteen-year-old strawberry roan Quarter horse cross and she was huge. When I was finally allowed to ride her, it was like sitting in an overstuffed easy chair that moved. She would stand perfectly still as I scrambled to get on her back. My brothers always saddled and bridled Dolly, but I soon found that those items of tack weren't necessary. Bareback was the style Dolly loved, and a halter and lead rope were all I needed to steer her in the right direction.

On Saturday mornings, I would rush to finish my chores so that I could put on my western outfit with the fringe, buckle my six guns around my skinny waist and head for the barn. My mother always packed a fine lunch for me and although she always included carrots or apples, Dolly ended up eating part of my meal. I have not met another horse in my lifetime that liked peanut butter and jelly sandwiches. What I ate, Dolly ate.

We would set out into the hills, safe within our fences, for a day of exploring and hiding out from the Indians or ambushers who lurked somewhere in my vivid imagination. When we had safely secured the area, Dolly would graze and I would lie back and study the beautiful Carolina blue skies. Dolly was an extremely good listener and as the bond between us grew, she heard a lot about my life's experiences. She was truly my best friend, and I enjoyed great times with her.

I would spend hours grooming Dolly, only to be upset because my father then used her to plow the fields. But as he explained to me in the nicest way he could, if you lived on the farm, you had to earn your keep. In my child's eyes, giving me rides and playing with me fulfilled her obligations, but my father didn't see it that way. So, off they would go, plowing or driving or whatever, until he said, "time for lunch." That phrase was intended for the humans working in the fields, not the horses. He soon learned that Dolly was very wise; she knew exactly what that meant. She would immediately pull my father and whatever implement to which she was attached back to the barn with very little effort. It wasn't too long after that my father started using more discreet ways to signal lunch breaks.

Even though I was a tried-and-true cowgirl, I still had times when girlish fads interested me. I was eight years old when I received the latest craze for Christmas – a Tiny Tears doll, complete with wardrobe. She was my absolute pride and joy and I always took her on my Saturday outings with Dolly. One Saturday, I returned home from riding later than usual and went straight to the dinner table. I had forgotten about Tiny Tears, and at bedtime I remembered leaving her by the creek side on her blanket. I decided to wait until the morning to get her. Besides, it was springtime and Dolly was staying out at night. Tiny Tears would be safe with her.

The next morning I skipped breakfast and immediately ran to the place where I had left Tiny Tears. But she wasn't there; I started searching frantically. About fifty feet away I found poor Tiny Tears at the edge of the creek, face down in the water. Dolly was standing right beside her. I felt relief, then dismay, when I picked Tiny Tears up. Her entire head had been chewed, and I knew who had done it. Even after all these years I still feel guilty when I remember how I yelled at Dolly, screaming that I hated her for what she did. It didn't once occur to me that horses, like toddlers, will put everything in their mouths.

I ran crying to my father who had heard me shrieking and, thinking I was injured, had set out to meet me. What he said didn't make me feel better, but he was right. The whole incident was my fault for leaving Tiny Tears there in the first place. And as far as Dolly was concerned, she had no idea why I was yelling at her. Nevertheless, she had followed me home, and I ran to her and hugged her and told her that I was sorry. I hope she understood. But the great thing about horses is that they ask no questions and do not judge. They love unconditionally. She was still my best friend.

Life as we knew it came to an end when I was eleven years old. My father suffered a series of strokes, rendering him bedridden. Although my mother and brothers made a valiant effort to keep the farm above water, we were slowly sinking. My oldest brother had enlisted in the Air Force prior to my father's illness and my other brother was engaged to be married. My mother had to concentrate her energy on full-time care for my father. Even though I tried to help out as much as possible, I was only in the sixth grade and was too young to assume adult responsibilities. As his condition became terminal, the reality set in that we would have to stop farming – our livelihood. We had depended on the farm for income in the summer. That, along with the income from my father's construction business, kept us comfortable. Now we would have to sell the land, livestock, vehicles, implements, etc. Aside from the obvious need for money, there was no one to physically manage the farm.

Little by little, assets were liquidated. I remember vividly the day my oldest brother came into the barn and sat down beside me as I brushed Dolly. He searched for the right words. I finally had the courage to look him in the eye and I knew that Dolly, my one steady influence, was going away. How could I possibly let her go? And why would God do this to me? No one would ever love Dolly the way I did. I held on to Dolly for dear life, crying tears that I couldn't let my father see. I knew he was hurting, but I could not imagine the pain he felt at having to give up first his health, then his beloved farm and his ability to provide for his family. I vowed to never let him see me cry.

The day came when a close family friend came to take Dolly to her new home. He had walked the two miles to our house. We said our good-byes without tears, because there were none left to shed, and he led Dolly down the road. It amazed me that she didn't resist or put up a fight. I was hurt, thinking that Dolly didn't really love me after all. She willingly went to her new home without once looking back. But I learned years later that horses are followers and, with a kind hand to lead them, will follow willingly. The last image I remember of that terrible day is my father, sitting on the front porch in his wheelchair with tears streaming down his cheeks, raising his hand in a good-bye wave to Dolly.

I later learned that my father had turned down monetary offers for Dolly, instead placing her with the man he knew would make her last years special. And they were. He kept Dolly active by giving buggy rides to neighborhood children in the summer and sleigh rides in the winter. She enjoyed a very easy lifestyle and died peacefully when she was 34 years old. I visited Dolly from time to time over the years, and she always had a special twinkle in her eye for me, as I did for her.

No matter how many horses I may own in my lifetime, the place reserved in my heart for that one special horse belongs to dear Dolly . . . then, now and forever my inspiration. She was truly my best friend.

ဆုဗ

Chapter Two
A Dream Comes True

Dear Dolly, Do you remember when I was a little girl and I pretended to be Dale Evans? On Saturday mornings, I would persuade my mother to pack a hobo lunch for me and I would don my western outfit with the fringe, buckle on my six guns and head for the barn to meet you.

No need to bother with a saddle, Dolly. You were so patient to let a scrawny rider climb aboard, knocking bony knees into your sides. No complaints from you; perhaps you knew that you would be sharing whatever my mother had packed for me to eat.

We headed off into the pasture, under the blue Carolina sky, to hide under the trees from outlaws. When all was clear and, more importantly, when my stomach began to rumble, we feasted. Whatever I ate, you ate. I have not met another horse since you that liked peanut butter and jelly, but I'm sure there are others out there. You were always a good listener and you heard a lot about my trials and tribulations. Dolly, you were truly my best friend.

It was thinking of those days so long ago that led to the situation today. You know that I have been leasing Barnaby for over a year now, and I must admit that he has fulfilled me in my quest. I realized that I had been missing the freedom only riding a horse can bring, but I also knew that I would never quite mirror our days together. But I need more, and this is what I need to talk to you about.

A co-worker told me about an Arabian horse farm nearby. I grew up reading about horses and knew the history of the Arabian breed, so I called the owner and asked if I could visit the farm. The thought had crossed my mind that I could buy my own horse, sell my house and move to the country. Then I could ride whenever I wanted, and the driving time would be eliminated. At this point, all the work involved in horsekeeping completely eluded me.

I was hooked the minute I drove up to the farm and looked into the valley below. I counted ten Arabian horses grazing peacefully in the spring sunshine. What a sight they were! I sat there for the longest time and watched with envy. Could there possibly be anything more beautiful? (No reflection on you, Dolly.)

I drove to the house, expecting to find the owner, Kathryn, waiting for me. Instead, I heard her call from a beat-up old ranch truck. She was out riding the fenceline and said that she would be back shortly. She told me to make myself at home and I did – I headed straight for the barn. There, to my delight, I found five broodmares, each with a new foal. They were all interested in me; the broodmares to see if I had brought any food and the babies for no particular reason other than youthful inquisitiveness. At any rate, I got lots of horse kisses before Kathryn drove up.

Kathryn gave me a tour of her farm and told me about a horse named DSF Piccalilli (Lilli), a National Show Horse with three-quarter Arabian blood and a lot of bells and whistles as the horse world goes. What is most important to me, however, is that I buy a horse I can ride and have for a soul mate (but not like the relationship you and I had). The trainer who has been working with Lilli is bringing her back to the farm tomorrow and I am returning to see her then. Dolly, I'll try to be realistic about this horse business, but if you need to nudge me to give me a reality check, be my guest. I'll talk to you after I meet Lilli. 'Night, Dolly

ೞೲ

Dear Dolly, When I went to see Lilli today, Kathryn and the trainer met me at the stable. Something about the trainer made me feel at ease. Her name is Shelby and I think we are going to be great friends.

But let's talk about Lilli. You know me, Dolly. I fell in love with the horse immediately and forgot that it is not like buying a car. I have such limited knowledge and skills where riding and taking care of horses is concerned, because you were fifteen years old when Dad bought you for me. What a lifetime of experience you already possessed.

I tried not to show my excitement as I stood back and observed as Shelby expertly saddled and bridled Lilli and led her to the round pen. She put Lilli through her paces on a lunge line, asking her to walk, trot and canter on command. And Dolly, the horse listened to her. I noticed that the entire time she was executing Shelby's commands, Lilli kept one ear pricked in her direction, waiting for the next order. This all just blew me away.

Then it was my turn to ride Lilli. I have to say that the whole incident was totally unlike riding bareback on you. I just told you what to do and you did it. Barnaby was easy to handle, but he was also an older horse who was experienced in the ways of the world. Lilli was trained to feel the slightest touch of the hand and heel, and she moved so gracefully. Up until that moment, I had given little thought to "easy hands," which Kathryn and Shelby said I had. Now I had to start thinking about heels down, and other terms I heard Shelby use a lot, including "left rein, right rein". I hope to learn everything I can from her.

Kathryn mentioned that Lilli had been born on her farm, but that she had been sold the year before to a man who asked for terms. When he didn't make his payments as scheduled, Kathryn went to pick Lilli up and was appalled when she saw that the mare was skin and bones and spooked at everything she encountered. The man apparently didn't like to muck stalls and deduced that the less feed that went into a horse, the less he had to shovel. Imagine someone being so cruel to a horse, Dolly.

Kathryn had taken Lilli to Shelby and she had provided the nutrition and care she needed to thrive again. She said that Lilli's self-esteem was low initially, but she was responding well to Shelby's loving care. I told Kathryn that I appreciated her honesty in telling me this, because she didn't have to give me Lilli's entire history.

I told Kathryn that I would think about Lilli and call her tomorrow. That's why I'm talking to you tonight. I need some help here, Dolly. Dare I even think that it's possible to have a horse like you again? Or is this just a pipe dream? All I know is that when I ride, I feel no stress or worry from my chaotic life. And if I buy Lilli, maybe I can re-capture what it was so long ago that made me happy. I sometimes wonder if it is better to try to relive those times in your youth that made you happiest or to make new memories in the present. Boy, that's heavy. The real likelihood is that maybe I just want to be Dale Evans again . . .

Dolly, you think on this tonight and I will, too. I'll meet you tomorrow morning bright and early to decide on my future. You know the place. 'Night, Dolly

ഇന്ദ

Dear Dolly, With you looking over my shoulder, I became Lilli's new owner. Something just seems right with this decision. I'm not trying to experience déjà vu. It's just that I need her and I think she needs me. She's had a roller-coaster ride, sometimes being treated like a prima donna, and other times being starved and abused. So I really feel that it's a good match. I've been caught up in being independent and making my own way, and I haven't given a thought to anyone else except myself in a long time. Maybe it's time for me to make a change in my life.

I'm really excited to have a horse! Part of the excitement comes from the decision I made to breed Lilli to Shelby's stallion. Imagine having a little filly or colt! It would have been so much fun if you had been a momma, but you can sure watch over this one for me. You remember that I was not allowed to see farm babies being born when I was a child, so just the thought of being totally involved with the prenatal care and the birth is so exciting!

Lilli will be going home with Shelby to be bred and to train for another sixty days. I will go down to Shelby's barn on weekends until Lilli can come back here. Then I will board her with Kathryn and visit as often as I can. Kathryn has recently built a new boarding facility with a round pen, but the arena is not yet completed. In the meantime, I plan to learn everything I can about horse training so that I can continue Lilli's training myself when I bring her home. I have a lot of questions, but I am reading everything I can get my hands on.

I was thinking of you today while I shopped at our local tack store. Remember the old rope halter you wore when I rode you? No need for a bit with you! And most times I rode you bareback, completely without fear, as only a child can do. Now, as a novice, I shopped for a bridle and bit (per Shelby's specifications) and finally selected one that would complement Lilli's beautiful brown eyes. Then I chose a blue halter and saddle pad (to please Kathryn, who insisted that Lilli's color is blue). Last, I purchased a lovely western saddle that was custom-made for someone long ago. My father once told me that the best saddle you can get is a well-fashioned one that was used before you. That way all the kinks and newness are worn out.

It occurred to me as I shopped that I have never put a bit into a horse's mouth. I finally realize just how much you knew on your own. You even knew which way to turn before I asked.

And, if I even mentioned heading for the barn, you took me there with great swiftness! Now I must rely on my own abilities and I am a little scared, but also feeling great excitement and anticipation.

Today has been so much fun! I told all my friends about Lilli and they think I am absolutely crazy! What in the world will someone who spends all her time working do with a horse? Exactly! A lot of my time has been spent working because I didn't have anyone to share my time with, and now there's Lilli. Besides, I have spent many professional years preaching the benefits of time management. Now it's time to practice what I preach.

I also called my ex-husband Ron, who now lives in Nashville. You know I still like to use him as my sounding board. When I told him that I had just made a large purchase, I'm sure he thought I meant jewelry or a new car. I have been called the mall queen many times, and shopping is my specialty. But imagine his shock at hearing that "large purchase" meant a horse! He must have thought I'd gone mad, but typically he simply said, "Cool."

I bought a new book today at the tack store. Its title is "Understanding Your Horse", and it is about the body language, etc., of horses and how to recognize the signs. It is really interesting, but it says nothing about horses that eat the heads off Tiny Tears dolls.

Remember that? I left her down by the creek and I guess you were either curious or hungry. At any rate, I really hated you for that. I don't know what behavior pattern you demonstrated that day, but I doubt if this book has a chapter on it. Anyway, I got over that incident years ago, and I learned not to leave things lying around.

Well, Dolly, I am going to go to sleep now and dream of my first weekend with Lilli. I know you're up there in greener pastures, but can you look down on us as we start our new life together? I need all the help I can get. 'Night, Dolly

ဆဩ

My decision to purchase Lilli was based on my feelings and intuition. I think it's very important to enlist the aid of those who are experts in judging whether a horse is right for you. The following list will detail some of the important features to consider before you purchase a horse:

- ⚘ Know what your arrangements will be as far as keeping the horse, whether stabled at home, boarded out, etc. Make certain that this is decided before you go looking.

- ⚘ Arrive early for your appointment with the owner so that you can observe the horse in his stall. Look for any signs of weaving, chewing on wood or pawing.

- ⚘ Ask the owner if you can see how the horse leads, ties, etc. If the horse is pasture kept, check to see if he is wearing a halter. That could indicate he is difficult to catch. As a matter of safety, horses should not wear halters in the pasture. Observe the owner catching the horse and his response. Does the horse pin his ears or does he willingly allow the haltering? Is he aggressive toward the owner or other horses?

- ⚘ Saddle the horse yourself to see how he behaves. Does he stand still or does he balk or fidget when you place the saddle on his back or when the girth is tightened? The horse should accept the bit willingly. If you are new at doing this, it is all right to ask the owner for help.

- ⚘ Ride the horse to see how he responds to your cues. You should also ask what the horse has been used for and what disciplines he is trained in. If at all possible, ask a trainer for an expert opinion.

- ⚘ Always have a vet check a horse before you purchase him. A complete exam should help you avoid costly medical expenses in the future. Unforeseen injuries or illnesses may occur, but the vet can advise you of any defects before you buy.

- ⚘ Take time to consider all your options. Don't let a lot of sales talk get in the way of making the right decision based on your needs. And if you don't feel good about what you're doing, chances are there is a good reason. Listen to your inner self.

Dear Dolly, Guess what? Lilli's going to have a baby! When I arrived at Shelby's to work with Lilli, a picture from the ultrasound was pinned to the stall door. I was so excited, even though someone had to pinpoint the location of the baby on the photo. I was the same way when I had my first daughter – I could in no way see what they were talking about on the ultrasound. But I am really looking forward to the next ten months or so.

Lilli doesn't seem to care whether she's pregnant or not. When I hugged her and congratulated her, she pinned her ears at me. You know, I can't remember a single time you pinned your ears at me, but I'm certain you wanted to many times. I hope this doesn't become a standard for Lilli.

Well, my day was filled with fun and frustration! Today was my first opportunity to actually put a saddle on Lilli. I can still hear Dad saying that was man's work, or I was too little – he always had some excuse for not letting me do it. Of course, with you, Dolly, there was no need for all that fancy stuff. At any rate, I now know just how much I have to learn if I want to be an independent horsewoman.

I told you a little about Shelby, the trainer who is schooling Lilli. She is an excellent trainer and I have really enjoyed the first 30 days of our time together before I take Lilli back to Asheville. It took me a while to catch on to her methods, but every time she wants me to get comfortable with a situation, she calmly announces that she has to run back to the house for a minute. This is what she did this morning and this is what happened while she was gone.

To begin with, I put Lilli's new blue halter on backward. When I finally got that right, I put her new blue saddle pad on. As I turned around to get the saddle, Lilli casually threw the saddle pad on the floor. This happened three times, but on the fourth, I guess Lilli had tired of the game and allowed the pad to stay on. The saddle gave me no problem, except that I must work on developing my biceps so that I can really tighten that girth!

As I was about to put the bit into Lilli's mouth (a little apprehensively, I must confess), Shelby walked back into the barn and tackled the task. Lilli seemed to be on her best behavior when Shelby was around, so I thought it best not to say anything about the saddle pad incident. I really felt relieved that I didn't have to bridle Lilli! I suppose when you grow up with a horse that gets ridden in a halter and is very seldom bitted, you get spoiled.

Shelby then took Lilli to the round pen to warm her up. She said that she likes the John Lyons' method of training and suggested that I buy some of his videos, which I did. At this point, I think it must be easy to train horses! At least, it looks easy on the videos. But I decided to watch Shelby first and gain from her experience. She put Lilli through her paces, turning her on command, sometimes even without words. It was fascinating to watch the control she had over Lilli. Then all too soon, it was my turn.

Dolly, I felt really confident as I stepped into the arena and faced my horse for the first time. I must say that I was impressed with what I had learned. Lilli performed beautifully and listened with one ear cocked toward me. She was great! Don't get me wrong; I don't think what Lilli did would ever compare to you standing at the other end of the long pasture, across creeks and meadows, heeding my call of "Dolly, dinner!" Lickety split, with the sound of hooves pounding the ground, you were there! No, it is not the same caliber of training, but those were the good old days and we are living in different times. I think that Lilli and I will do just fine in our new life together.

The riding lesson went well, except for one minor incident. I was on Lilli and Shelby was in the middle of the arena, watching me. She always wears a baseball cap over her ponytail. Suddenly, a gust of wind came along and the cap flew off, barely touching Lilli's foreleg. Lilli spooked and started running. Although I was caught completely off guard, I miraculously stayed on!

Shelby is a very laid-back person and she views every catastrophe as a learning experience. Her comment was, "I'm so glad that happened. Now let's fix it." She had me dismount and she retrieved the cap. Then she placed it in the middle of the arena, about twenty feet away from us. She asked me to lead Lilli toward the cap until the mare was close enough to touch it. I did this as Shelby calmly told Lilli, "It's okay, come here. Now I want you to see what you got so upset over." Lilli produced the expected Arabian snort a couple of times and then let Shelby touch the cap all over her body. The last place it landed was on Lilli's head. I had to snap a picture of that.

After we worked in the round pen, Shelby and I took our horses on the trail by her farm. That's what I want Lilli to be: a good trail horse. So far, she's very calm when we are riding away from the arena, but she is still nervous when I ride her "fenced in". I don't know what that indicates, but Shelby says that if I am nervous, Lilli will also be because she can feel my muscles tense. Makes sense to me, so I'll have to breathe more often and try to loosen up when I'm in the arena. It is likely because I had such a great experience with Barnaby that I am very relaxed on the trail.

Dolly, I hope you don't grow tired of hearing about another horse. You know my heart belongs to you. Every time I learn something new about Lilli, it jogs my memory and I think of the special times we had way back then. I wouldn't trade our time together for the world.

I am going to the laundry room now; I need to smell my riding clothes one more time before I turn in. 'Night, Dolly

ଫାଓ୍ଷ

The methods of de-spooking horses that are used by the trainer with whom I work are very effective:

ଓ୍ଷ After saddling the horse and leading him to the round pen, she takes two empty feed sacks tied together with twine and rubs them over the horse's body, including the legs. Initially, the horse will try to run away, but he usually will become comfortable with the sacks touching his body and accept them without spooking. Then the trainer secures the sacks across the horse at the withers, placing one sack on each side of the horse.

ɕ Next she puts the horse through his paces, whether it is in a round pen or on a lunge line. This way the horse gets used to the sack flapping in the wind when he moves. Once the trainer feels comfortable that the horse has accepted the sacks, she stops the horse, removes the sacks and places them on the ground.

ɕ The horse is then asked to walk across the sacks. It usually takes several efforts to get the horse to step straight across with all four feet. When she is successful, the trainer repeats the lesson from the other direction. She makes this a part of her normal routine with any horse prior to riding.

ɕ After the horse is totally at ease with the sacks, plastic tarps can be utilized, or poles or trash cans. The goal is to have any noise or visual distraction that could spook a horse become second nature while introduced in a controlled environment.

ৼᢙ

Chapter Three
Let The Games Begin

Dear Dolly, Are you up there? I really need your advice. Today Lilli came to live at the barn where I am boarding her. I was so excited to get her back after sixty days of training and trail riding at Shelby's. Sure, the time with Shelby gave me a chance to learn things I didn't know about horsekeeping and riding, but I was very anxious to have Lilli home where I could see her every day instead of only on weekends.

I called the manager at the barn to let her know that I would be out shortly after work to visit Lilli. Somehow, I must have miscommunicated my wishes, because when I arrived, Lilli was not in her stall. No one was around the barn, so I set out to search for my pride and joy, only to find her grazing contentedly in the pasture with two other horses. "No problem," I thought to myself. I retrieved Lilli's halter and lead rope and entered the pasture, closing the gate behind me. Now, I had seen Shelby bring Lilli in from the pasture at her barn lots of times and it seemed very easy. If I remember correctly, all I needed to do to catch *you* was call your name and you obliged without the need for restraint. Somehow I expected it to be the same way with Lilli. I was *wrong!*

I slowly walked toward Lilli with the halter in my hand and everything was fine until I got about three feet away. I could see her looking at me out of the corner of her eye. Suddenly she ran away, stopping about twenty feet from me. Again I tried, with the same result. After about thirty minutes of chasing Lilli (and her friends) all over the pasture, I gave up. Now, from reading about horses I know that Lilli won the battle, but I also knew I didn't have a chance of catching her. I left the barn totally dejected, and as I drove away I could swear I saw Lilli giving me a victory smile.

Dolly, I was so disappointed because this was the first time I had a chance to have Lilli all to myself and I blew it. I called the barn manager and asked her to make sure that Lilli was kept in her stall the next day so that she wouldn't be able to pull the same stunt again. I planned to zero in on the problem of catching Lilli in the pasture later, but right now I was very anxious to get started with Lilli, without Shelby present. It was my turn to show what I could do.

The next day I went straight to the barn after work and this time Lilli was in her stall as I had requested. When she saw me, Lilli walked to the back of the stall and turned away from me. I was crushed! Here I was, ready to give my body and soul, not to mention my wallet, to this horse, and she was playing me like a chump. I offered her a carrot and placed her halter around her head. Now I had a new best friend; Lilli began nuzzling and flashing those baby browns at me. I figured this would be the right time to groom her. I found out that she is a vain creature, and rightfully so – her bay coat gleams and her mane falls below her shoulders. As I groomed Lilli, I talked to her about my day, and she nuzzled me gently. "This is the life," I thought.

Then I placed the saddle pad on Lilli's back. She did exactly the same thing she did at Shelby's barn; she threw off the pad each time I turned my back on her. After five or six attempts, Lilli grew bored and settled down. I placed the saddle on her back and you would have thought I had loaded a tractor on her. She threw her head, looked around and gave a loud snort. She tossed and turned and stomped. I was frazzled by this time, but little by little, I managed to get the cinch tightened without bodily harm to the horse or myself. Then, unlike the time Shelby had bailed me out, it was time to place the bit in Lilli's mouth.

I know I was spoiled when I was young, because I didn't have to learn any of this with you. Now I really wished that I had learned this basic skill back then. Although I was a novice at bitting, I had seen it done and had practiced it in my sleep. "Piece of cake," I thought. *Not!* All my life I have heard that horses instinctively know when a human is nervous and that proved so true. Lilli put her head down on command, but the minute I placed the bridle near her head, she raised it to just above my reach. "Just calm down," I said to myself, "You know how to do this." Again and again I tried, with the same result. Lilli was toying with me and I grew more frustrated by the minute. Here I had made the decision to make Lilli my new life's partner and she was taking full advantage of my kindness. I was devastated.

Finally, I decided that the only way to get Lilli bridled was to put a halter on her and place the bridle over it. This was a temporary fix, I realized, but I had to show Lilli that she could not get away with this behavior. I remember hearing my Dad say that it is very important that the human wins battles – if a horse gets one over on you, it is likely to happen every time. So we eventually made it to the round pen and I lunged Lilli just as I had been taught. I rode her without incident, but the bridling catastrophe left me rattled. I've come home to read some more before going to bed; tonight I will practice bitting in my sleep. It sure is easy to do that way.

I do know one thing: life was a lot simpler when I was five and you were fifteen. If you come up with any bright ideas, send them my way, please. In the meantime, I'm going to soak in a nice, hot tub and pretend I'm riding Lilli across the meadow. She'll have a bit in her mouth in my dream. 'Night, Dolly

ଝଓଔ

Horses have a natural instinct to keep away from danger, which is why you have to earn their trust. Humans are a potential threat until a horse approves of them. If you want to catch a horse in the pasture, you have to prove that you are not a threat, but rather an ally. I know how discouraged I was when I tried to catch Lilli and couldn't get her to trust me. The following steps will be helpful when you attempt to catch an elusive horse:

- ଔ Approach the horse slowly from his left side, holding the halter behind your back. Talk to the horse to warn him of your approach so that he is not frightened if he doesn't see you until you are close to him.

- ଔ A horse has a comfort zone of about ten feet that humans commonly refer to as our "space." When you reach that distance, stop and let the horse acknowledge you. He will probably do this by raising his head. Usually, he will want to see if you have brought anything to eat, so perhaps have a treat with you. Give the horse the treat, and if he moves away, reposition yourself and wait.

- ଔ Without making any sudden moves, bring the halter slowly into view and lay the lead rope over his neck. Usually, this will be enough to make the horse feel restrained and he will not try to move away from you.

- ଔ Put the halter on and fasten it slowly so as not to startle the horse, then take a minute to pet him and praise him. Walk forward slowly, but remember not to wrap the lead rope around your hand (ever!). The horse may still try to run away and will pull you with him.

- ଔ Remember to be patient. If you are in a hurry and show it, you may not be as successful as you would like.

Dear Dolly, Do you have fond memories of the times you pulled a wagon full of vacation bible school kids to church? I certainly do. We even loaded our dog, Scout, onto the back of the wagon. You proceeded with the precious cargo and willingly tolerated the tugs and pulls you got as they stepped down and gave you thank-you hugs. We tied your lead rope to the tree beside the church and you waited patiently until we were ready for the trip back home.

I had hoped for this same kind of camaraderie with Lilli. No matter which of us was in charge, you and I were in complete sync. I excitedly started this day with a new outlook and was eager to continue working with Lilli.

On this occasion, I groomed Lilli for an extra long time before placing the saddle pad on her back. Much to my surprise, she accepted it without objection. The saddle also went on smoothly. My hands were sweating as I picked up Lilli's bridle. *She knew it!* She had saved all the game-playing for the bit! I had the same problem as before, but this time Lilli threw her head. I had to do something, so I went to the tack room and got a mounting block and tried to put the bit in her mouth from a more elevated position. But the taller I got, the taller Lilli got. I'd be willing to bet *you* were up there laughing!

An experienced horsewoman who boards her horse in the stall next to me came to my aid. "Let me show you how this works. It won't take a minute," she said. "Lilli knows you're having trouble and she's using it to her advantage." Then the woman proceeded to demonstrate exactly how to expertly put a bit in a horses' mouth. It was not to be! For thirty minutes she tried with the same result that I, a mere novice, had achieved. She finally gave up and said, "This horse is hopeless. You need to sell her and get another horse."

Frustrated, I got into my car and called Shelby. I told her that I would gladly give Lilli to her and keep the foal when it was born. She could hear the desperation in my voice and asked me to relay the events as they had happened. Shelby said that as much as she appreciated my generous offer of giving her this fabulous, expensive horse, she wanted to try another approach first. She asked me to come to her barn as soon as I could. I told her to expect me shortly.

When I arrived, Shelby told me that the problem I was having was not a physical one, but rather a psychological one. To prove her point, she had me bridle every horse in the place, including her mule. Dolly, I was so excited! I realized then that *Lilli* was the problem, not me. She was very smart and realized how nervous I was. She had decided to test me – and she had won. But I had learned a valuable lesson along the way. I was perfectly capable of bridling a horse and I had a bone to pick with Lilli. I headed straight back to the barn, arriving shortly after dusk.

I found Lilli resting leisurely in her stall, waiting for the carrot she assumed I had brought for her. I didn't have one – but I *did* have a bridle and bit. I walked into her stall as though I was ten feet tall, told Lilli to put her head down and immediately slipped the bit in her mouth without so much as a lead rope for restraint. Lilli looked as though she had seen a ghost. I'm sure she asked herself, "Who *is* this woman?" Let me tell you, Dolly. I have had many successes in business, but nothing compared to the feeling I got when that bridle went on without a hitch. I vowed to never have this problem again. What a relief!

Dolly, it just goes to show you that what I read is true: a horse can sense even the slightest apprehension in humans. Lilli is proving to be a real challenge. My life with you did not prepare me for this! Even though I had a weak moment today when I wanted to give Lilli away, I am not a quitter.

Tomorrow will be a better day. Dolly, I felt your presence when I walked back into that stall. I know you are looking out for me, but you can't be with me all the time. After all, what is the use of having perpetual green grass up there if you can't enjoy it! 'Night, Dolly

ꟷ

I read "how to" books countless times before I tried to bridle Lilli. Although I knew the method, I was nervous and it showed. The following technique will tell you how to successfully bridle a horse. But before you do, breathe.

- Slip the horse's halter off his muzzle and slide it back around his neck. Standing to the left of the horse, put your right arm under the horse's jaw and hold the cheek pieces of the bridle together in front of his face. Rest the bit on your left hand, just under the muzzle.

- Move the bridle gently up the horse's face. When the bit touches the horse's mouth, insert your thumb gently between the lips at the corner so that it presses slightly on the gum in the gap between the horse's teeth. The horse will open his mouth instinctively.

- Bring the headpiece up over the horse's ears, taking care not to let the bit drop out of the horse's mouth. Carefully fit both ears between the browband and the headpiece, and check that all of the horse's forelock is lying free over the browband.

- Fasten the throatlatch first, so that if the horse pulls away from you he will not pull the bridle off. Fasten it loosely so as not to interfere with the horse's breathing.

To remove the bridle:

- ☙ Fasten a halter loosely around the horse's neck. Undo the throatlatch. Taking hold of the headpiece in one hand, pull the bridle gently over the ears, and lower the bridle slowly down the front of the horse's face. The horse will ease the bit out of his mouth by himself.

- ☙ Do not pull the bridle off too quickly and bang the bit against the horse's teeth. This may cause the horse to be resistant to accepting the bit in the future.

Dear Dolly, Well, you'd never guess what happened today! You were definitely on my mind as I headed for the barn to visit Lilli on July 4th. The holiday denotes freedom and that is exactly what you were to me. You gave me the freedom to ride across the meadow with the wind in my face and the freedom to forget that I was just a little girl who lived in a boy's world. (You know, where boys could do anything and girls could cook and clean.) But that's another story; I still feel anger about how I was raised to believe that girls could do very little except look pretty.

This particular July 4th I was eager to celebrate my freedom with Lilli. I set my sights on having a lovely day working on my riding skills. I knew there would be very little activity around the barn early in the morning. Asheville always has a parade and many downtown restaurants celebrate by joining street vendors for a "taste of the town." I wasn't surprised that I was the only horse mother visiting the barn.

I saddled and bridled Lilli without any mishaps (doesn't that sound good?) and walked her to the round pen. The ground work started out fine; I put Lilli into a trot, canter and then back to a walk. I was practicing turning Lilli at certain points of the round pen when she suddenly picked up the pace; I asked her to walk and instead she began to gallop around the round pen. It was the first time I had seen Lilli out of control during groundwork. Then I noticed that the saddle had slipped and was hanging sideways on her. No wonder she was panicked!

Well, Dolly, the only thing to do at that moment was to get out of there. So I went to the fence and sat on the highest rail, all the while trying to calm Lilli. I was amazed to see that even though the saddle was now upside down, Lilli continued to run against the rail as a properly trained John Lyons student should. I kept saying, "Easy, Lilli, easy Lilli" until she began to take heed. Then as suddenly as she had bolted, she came to a halt.

The temperature was already near ninety degrees and very humid. Lilli was dripping wet and the veins had popped out on her body. She snorted and blew and let me know in no uncertain terms that I had messed up big-time today. Now that Lilli had calmed down, I walked back into the round pen and inspected the saddle, immediately noticing what had happened. Initially I had thought that maybe I hadn't tightened the girth strap enough, but I remembered checking it just before we left the barn.

What Shelby had warned me about had come true. She had told me that I needed to see about replacing a worn girth strap on the saddle. However, I didn't replace it soon enough and Lilli paid the price.

Luckily, Lilli wasn't injured, but she kept her ears pinned at me the rest of the morning. I'm ashamed to admit that I felt relieved that I had to leave without riding Lilli. Where is that coming from, Dolly? On the way home I stopped at the saddle shop to have the strap replaced and the others checked for fraying. I just wish I had taken Shelby's advice sooner.

Well, Dolly, as soon as everything seems to be coming together for this horse and me, some unforeseen obstacle pops up. Didn't I take you for granted? If Lilli and I can be half the team that you and I were, I will be a happy woman. I so want to make a difference in this horse's life and I want her to make a difference in mine.

Dolly, you were always a wise old soul. Help me find some way to be a better horsewoman, please. In the meantime, I'm going to watch a video about Black Beauty and maybe pick up some pointers myself. 'Night, Dolly

I learned a valuable lesson about checking buckles, girths, straps and cinches.

- ൪ Basically, check anywhere that metal meets leather, because that is where the most stress occurs. Replace any equipment that shows even the smallest sign of fraying.

- ൪ Check reins and bridle for wear and cracking and make certain that any screws or buckles are securely tightened.

- ൪ Make it a habit to check your saddle and bridle before you mount the horse.

- ൪ Clean and condition your tack regularly. Don't let the leather get dry and brittle. Tack should be cared for even if you don't ride regularly.

- ൪ If possible, change the holes that you buckle on the girth, breastplate or bridle. This will distribute the stress more evenly and save wear and tear. But make certain that doing so does not result in too loose of a fit, jeopardizing the safety of the horse and rider.

Dear Dolly, Do you remember the little pep talk we had recently about trying to think of ways for me to become a better horsewoman? Well, just when I thought I might be turning it all around, I made a really stupid mistake.

I actually thought we were on the right track, Dolly. Lilli and I had a great ride today. Her groundwork was excellent as always and I rode her first in the round pen and then in the arena. I asked Lilli to canter up the hill leading from the round pen and I felt in control again. It felt good to have a session go smoothly.

When I got back to the barn, I decided not to give Lilli her usual bath. The weather had turned cool and windy, so I just let her stand inside the barn tacked up during the cool down.

Some people were visiting the barn to inquire about boarding their horses there. I told them how great the atmosphere was and they commented about what a beautiful horse I had. I beamed with pride! "It doesn't get any better than this," I thought to myself.

Thank goodness the visitors had already left with the stable manager, because they would have seen quite a spectacle! I don't know what possessed me, but instead of taking Lilli's saddle off first, I removed the bridle. *What was I thinking?*

Dolly, what would you have done if you had the choice between standing in the wash stall of a barn or heading for green grass? You'd do exactly what Lilli did. She left me standing with the bridle in my hand and went off to calmly graze without me. "No problem," I thought. "I'll just let her graze for a while and then I'll bring her in." I thought we had developed a close relationship by now and she would be easy to catch.

Lilli had other ideas when her grazing time was up. She repeated the whole routine that she pulled on me much earlier in our relationship. Each time I would get close to her, she would meander over a few yards in the other direction. There was real concern on my part, because Kathryn had not fenced the property yet. It is very close to a main road, and I worried that Lilli might run into traffic. On a hunch, I inched toward the paddock where Lilli's friend, Spring, was grazing. As I approached the gate, Spring called out and Lilli's ears perked up. She trotted over to the paddock and asked to be let in. I very gladly obliged, because the last thing I wanted was to chase her up to the main road. I know it wasn't the correct way to solve the problem, but it worked for me.

So, Dolly, the moral of this story is: everything in its right order. Always remove the saddle before you remove the bridle. You can bet that won't happen again. See, that comes from growing up with an older horse that knows the ropes. Not once did you ever run away, Dolly. I guess you were pretty satisfied with the life you had, huh?

It appears that this horsekeeping stuff is harder than they indicate in those books. Every day I learn something new, and at my age that is quite an achievement. Tomorrow I'm sure Lilli will teach me something else, but tonight I'm going to feel sorry for myself. I wish I were Dale Evans. 'Night, Dolly

&OCB

Dear Dolly, Has a horse ever stepped on your foot? Probably not, but Lilli stepped on mine today. The worst part was that she looked off into the horizon and I could almost hear her humming softly. I said, "Excuse me, Lilli, but I think that's my foot you're on." She didn't budge. I tried pulling her off balance with the lead rope, but that didn't work. Finally, I realized that if I pushed her hindquarters, she would move away from me. Thank goodness my brain kicked in. Boy, my foot smarts!

Today I rode Lilli down by the creek. The lady who owns Spring rode her beside me and we had a great time. Lilli is happiest when she is on the trail, and I wish there were more around the barn. I've been thinking a lot lately about the idea of selling my house and buying one with facilities to keep Lilli. Thinking back to my childhood again, Dolly, there is nothing quite like waking up in the morning (or middle of the night for that matter) and walking out to the barn to be greeted by your very own horse.

Dolly, I know you were alone a lot of the time. You didn't have your own baby to raise. The reason I'm bringing this up is that I have thought a lot about Lilli being alone, and although I originally wanted to sell her foal, I'm giving serious thought to keeping it for Lilli to raise. What do you think of that? Would that make a difference?

Kathryn told me that Lilli is an excellent mother and dotes on her babies, so it makes sense to me that if that would make Lilli happy, then she will hopefully cooperate a little more with me. Sometimes she can be so good, but just when I think we're making progress, she starts to act up. I hope the longer she knows me, the more she will trust me.

As far as the foal is concerned, Kathryn has told me that she would be glad to take over the attendant duties when Lilli delivers. She has an apartment over the barn where she sleeps during foaling season, which allows her to keep a close eye on the pregnant mares. Naturally, I would want to be there for the birth, but she cautioned me that once labor starts, the birth is so fast that I probably wouldn't get to the barn in time to witness it. That depresses me, because I wasn't allowed to see births on the farm growing up. I really want to be there when this foal is born.

Dolly, I know you've heard me talk about my ex-husband who lives in another city. Yesterday, I talked with Ron on the phone and he wants to meet Lilli. He is a man who has only ridden a horse once in his life and he admits to being terrified of them. But, just as he was in our marriage, if it makes me happy to own a horse even though he thinks I'm stark raving mad, he's all for it. Ron is planning to come to town next week for Bele Chere, a street festival that we attend together every year, and I'm taking him to the barn for an introduction to Lilli. Maybe I can even persuade him to ride her. Wish me luck!

The phone is ringing, so I must go for now. Sleep well up there in the meadow and continue to look in my direction when you wake. 'Night, Dolly

℘℃ℨ

I had a lot to learn about taking care of Lilli during her pregnancy. I read everything I could to help me prepare, but I found that a visit from the veterinarian is the best place to start. This list contains tips from the vet who attended Lilli:

  ℭ Normal gestation for mares can be anywhere from 330 to 350 days, with the average being 332. It is very important to make certain that your mare receives adequate prenatal care from the outset. Begin with a complete examination by your veterinarian.

  ℭ The mare should receive proper nutrition. For the first eight months, feed her normal rations, but during the last ninety days, gradually double her grain intake (but no more than 14% protein). Also, add increased amounts of clean, well-cured green alfalfa hay. Hay must be completely free of mold for the duration of the pregnancy and for the last 90 days, the mare must not consume any fescue grass or hay. Fescue has been proven to cause abortion or septicemia in foals.

೮ Adequate turnout in the fresh air and sunshine is vital for a healthy pregnancy. If at all possible, pregnant mares should be turned out together. Injuries can occur when they are placed with high-spirited horses.

೮ In addition to the regular vaccination and de-worming program your veterinarian recommends, a pregnant mare will need to be vaccinated against Rhinopneumonitis, an upper respiratory infectious disease. Vaccinations should be given in the fifth, seventh and ninth months of gestation.

ಜೂ಼

Chapter Four
Auja Maria, My Soulmate

Dear Dolly, Guess who was on the phone? It was Shelby, calling to let me know that she has a beautiful black Arabian mare that she wants to sell. Her name is Auja Maria and she is eight years old. She bought Maria from some people who kept her in the pasture for their grandchildren to pet. Maria had never been ridden, but Shelby rode her for the first time bareback. In fact, the first time she took Maria on the trail, she ponied her, but halfway through the ride, she returned the lead horse to the barn and rode Maria out by herself. Shelby would like me to ride Maria next weekend to show me that all Arabians aren't as unpredictable as Lilli.

At this point I don't know if I want to ride Maria. Right now, I am discouraged with my relationship with Lilli and I might be looking for an excuse to blame her for every bad thing that has happened. The truth is, I have made some really big mistakes with Lilli and she has used them against me. She's a very clever horse, that one. But I will go and look at Maria, because I might know someone who would be interested in buying her.

Well, Dolly, go back to sleep. I'm sorry that I woke you, but I don't suppose you need a lot of sleep. Why don't you indulge in some night grazing since you're awake anyhow and I'll talk to you after I see Maria. 'Night, Dolly

ଊଓ

Dear Dolly, You know me well. Did you believe me for a minute when I said that I didn't know if I would ride Maria? The instant I saw her, I knew. She is really beautiful in an Arabian sort of way. Not big and muscular like you, but small and compact, with lots of power. She appears to be a very laid-back, relaxed mare.

Sometimes when I close my eyes and try really hard, I can hear the sound of your whinny. Maria sounds a lot like you with her soft, low-pitched whinny. Could she possibly be the soul mate I've been longing for, Dolly?

I rode Maria halfway through the trail ride and Shelby rode one of her horses. Then we traded horses on the way back to the barn. As much as I love to ride Lilli when she's behaving, Maria's canter is the best I've encountered – that rocking chair canter you hear so much about. She is a very easy ride and she keeps her head low even before I ask for it.

Lilli has this spirited walk with lots of energy. Maria is slow and deliberate. The two are exact opposites. I don't know how they will get along, but Maria is the newest member of my family. Have I lost my sanity? Maybe Shelby was really trying to sell her to me without being obvious. She kept saying that she wasn't trying to get me to buy her. I don't know if that was actually Shelby's intention, but I am very happy with Maria. I can't wait to get her to the barn. She has sixty days' free training and Shelby threw in a free breeding with the purchase. I will visit Maria the same way I did Lilli and stagger my time between the two. I have also accrued lots of vacation time that I didn't have a reason to take before, so I intend to make good use of it. I have purpose to my life now.

I only did one stupid thing that I'm aware of today. Upon returning from our trail ride, I felt so confident on Maria's back that without thinking, I rode her straight into the barn. "Stop!" Shelby yelled. "You could get killed doing that. What if she reared right now? Then you would hit your head on the ceiling." I backed Maria right out, feeling chastised, and rightfully so.

I can't wait to tell Ron that I now own not one, but *two* horses. I don't think he has recovered from the initial shock of hearing that I bought Lilli, but now Maria? He is considering riding Lilli when he visits, so I'm looking forward to seeing that. Be an angel on the ceiling and get his reaction to Maria, will you, Dolly?

Sometimes I long to once again see the open fields where you used to roam. Have you forgotten them? I hope not, because

I haven't. Well, I'm giving serious thought to finding some fields of my own. Now that I have two horses, it's time. Maybe I'll ask Ron's opinion on that when he visits next weekend.

He called again last night and said that the idea of riding horses is becoming very important to him. In fact, he says that he can't wait to ride Lilli. What a challenge! But then again, he lived with me for a long time, so he's used to challenges.

Shelby suggested that I ship Lilli back to her barn so that both horses would be together. At first I didn't think that would be a good idea, but considering the lack of open space for trails at the current location, plus the facilities available at Shelby's, I think it might be a smart move. I don't know if Lilli and Maria will get along with each other, but I know that horses are social animals. The thought of having just one horse doesn't interest me because I want them to be companions. You know what it's like to be alone.

I'm going to give careful consideration to moving Lilli to Shelby's barn. Go back to the pastures above Rainbow Bridge, Dolly, and have a little clover for me. 'Night, Dolly

೫෮ೲ

Dear Dolly, I'd have to say that today was a learning experience. The weather was perfect and Shelby decided that we would take a long trail ride. Maria and I rode past a lot of obstacles and she didn't spook at any of them. We even crossed a one-lane bridge that was very high above the water. So you can understand that I was very complacent and confident in my horse's docile nature as we turned toward Shelby's farm. To say that I was relaxed was an understatement, Dolly. It kind of reminded me of the way I rode you without thinking. That's what I've missed with Lilli. You constantly have to think before she acts. It's a different story with Maria.

Without any warning, Maria suddenly shot out from under me and I started my downward slide. Would you believe I didn't have my feet in the stirrups? I tried to maneuver for the fall and managed to land on my tailbone. Luckily, I only suffered humiliation as a result of the fall. Shelby jumped off and asked if I was all right. She insisted that this was totally unlike Maria and I agreed, so we tried to determine what had happened to her.

Shelby examined Maria all over and her right hind leg had a swollen area that she believed was a hornet or yellow jacket's sting. Whatever it was, Maria had reacted quickly and taught me that I should *always* keep my feet in the stirrups when riding. So, Dolly, that's another lesson I learned the hard way. (Believe me, that dirt road was *very* hard.) Tonight, I intend to sit in a hot tub and nurse my wounded ego.
'Night, Dolly

ଽଉଓ

Part Two
A New Beginning

Chapter Five
The Birth Of Summerwind Farm

Dear Dolly, You have really big ears, so I know you already have a handle on what is happening. I'll tell you anyway, just in case you missed part of the conversation. Ron visited this weekend and we went to see Lilli. As promised, he actually rode her, although he admitted to being a little nervous. I snapped a picture to mark the occasion, but I don't know if I'll show it to anyone. Ron looked like a deer caught in the headlights. As the weekend drew to a close, we started talking about our past lives, the present and how we have missed being part of each other's future.

During the conversation, I mentioned to Ron that I was thinking of sending Lilli back to Shelby's so that I could board both horses together. I also mentioned that I was thinking about selling my house and buying another with a barn and pasture for Lilli and Maria. Can you believe what he said next?

He actually thinks we should buy a farm *together* and raise horses. He says that the idea of horses is growing on him. The problem is that with the land value here in North Carolina versus the land value where he lives in Tennessee, we could buy double the land there. That would mean me giving up my job and moving there. I don't know if I can do that. Certainly, the job is a huge part of what makes me who I am, but in all honesty, it is very demanding and stressful. That's why I got back into horses. When I ride, I think only of that moment, not some deadline or dilemma at the bank. It has become a way for me to relieve stress and is a welcome form of therapy.

It would also mean giving up a convenient relationship with Shelby. That means a lot to me, because she has taught me so much about riding already and I still have much to learn from her. I know we will visit each other, but no matter how good the intentions are, that is next to impossible with the demands of living in today's times. Plus, I grew up in North Carolina and although I have lived in other states, I miss my roots. I have a lot to consider.

Dolly, the most important part of this decision will stem on whether or not Ron and I can live peaceably. Our marriage was always in turmoil and we were constantly arguing. He viewed our relationship with optimism, insisting we had more good days than bad. I, on the other hand, looked at it oppositely. Could we possibly expect to live the rest of our days together and be happy? If we decide to remarry, would it be successful after we have lived separate lives for four years?

I mentioned this to Shelby today as we rode Lilli and Maria on the trail. It was our first outing since I moved Lilli back to her barn. She reined Lilli to an abrupt stop and said, "Do you know what the statistics are for people marrying each other a second time? Almost zero chance of making it work." Shelby's probably thinking that giving up a successful career, my home in the mountains and my roots here is absolutely crazy. And she's right, Dolly. I'd have to be out of my mind to even consider moving myself and everything I own to another state.

If I do this, I will have to find another job and start climbing the ladder again. Talk about career suicide! I don't know if I can face that. Wouldn't it be great if I didn't have to work if I do make this move? I don't think that would be possible financially, but what a dream! Imagine being able to walk out the back door in the morning with a steaming cup of coffee headed . . . where? To the barn to listen to the horses having their breakfast, of course. Wouldn't that be the life?

I feel like I did that time you and I ran away from home. Mother did something I didn't like (I must have been seven or eight) and I packed a hobo bag and announced that I was running away and never coming back. "Okay," she said, " but be sure to take a coat with you. The nights can get cold this time of year." That's it? After all this time as a family member, shouldn't someone have begged me not to go?

Obedient as you were and always up for an adventure, you followed me to the upper pasture where you grazed and I fumed and felt sorry for myself until dinnertime. I sat there and the longer I sat, the more I thought about the homemade buttermilk biscuits that Mother must be making right about now. Try as I might, I couldn't put that taste out of my mind.

Finally, as dark descended, I decided that since no one came looking for you or me, I would go back and show them that they couldn't keep me away. As I walked into the kitchen, I saw Mother putting a glass of milk at my place in the dining room. "Come on in," she said. "Dinner's just about ready." You know, Dolly, that was the best meal I ever tasted.

I feel as though I will be running away from home if I leave Asheville. I love this place so much, but Ron and I have a chance to build a life together. Maybe we've both grown up while we've been living apart. I know that in spite of everything that went wrong in our marriage, he is still the person I call when I need a friend or confidante. He's the first person I call when I need advice. Go figure.

Dolly, will I be running away? Does part of me yearn for the escape from my stressful and demanding job? Even though I like my independence, does a small part of me want to have someone to lean on? Without saying a word, you can help me make this decision, Dolly. Sleep on it. Talk to you tomorrow. 'Night, Dolly

ഔଓ

Dear Dolly, I took the day off work Friday and went to meet Shelby. She planned to work with Lilli more extensively and wanted me to be there. I still haven't decided whether or not to move to Tennessee, but Lilli does need more training and she and Maria are learning to tolerate each other.

Shelby's seventeen-year-old daughter, Ginny, has been exercising Lilli for me during the week and has had some trouble with her. Lilli isn't responding to cues from her. I haven't had many riding problems with Lilli, just the previous bit and saddle pad dilemmas.

Shelby rode Lilli with no incidents of memory lapse. But, as she pointed out, horses usually behave as they should with a trainer. I also rode Lilli and she was fine. I think Lilli thrives on being one step ahead of humans. In the back of my mind I was wondering if Lilli would dare to act up when Shelby was present.

Dolly, I've done a lot of thinking about the future. As secure as I feel living independently, a part of me would like to share my love for horses with someone else. It's funny, but after you were taken from me when Dad was sick, I said I never wanted to have another horse. I couldn't wait to grow up and get as far away from the farm as possible. And now here I am right back on the road to country life. I should have known better than to say never!

Ron called tonight to say that he is "kind of, sort of" looking for farms in his area so that we can compare prices to those here. I haven't looked at real estate here because I'm certain that as soon as I put my house on the market, it will sell. This area is very desirable (not for a horse, though), so I have to know where I'm going before I put a For Sale sign in the yard.

Tomorrow I'm going to visit Lilli and Maria again and see how they are doing together. I'm really excited to have them both in one place, and I'm even more excited about Lilli's baby that is due in April. But since I've moved Lilli, the midwife duties will take on a whole new direction. I don't know if Shelby will want to assume the responsibility and I hesitate to ask her.

If I decide to move to Tennessee, I will be completely responsible for the foaling, as would be the case if I stay here and buy another property. Dolly, that really doesn't help make the decision for me, does it?

I purchased a new John Lyons book that I'm going to start reading tonight while you graze the heavenly pastures under the stars. It's called "John Lyons on Horses." Until tomorrow, then. 'Night, Dolly

ଓଓଔ

Dear Dolly, If you eavesdrop at all – and I think you do – you have heard me talking to Ron about a property he has located. It has twelve acres and a five-year-old house (who cares about a house). There is only a pole shed on the property at this time, but it would make a suitable structure to add a barn to. Although Ron has no experience at barn building, he has been in the brick business for a long time and knows a lot about construction. The prospect of building a barn is both scary and exciting to him, and Ron is certain that his dad, brother and brother-in-law will help him if that's what we decide to do and this is the right property for us.

Dolly, I have accepted Ron's proposal that we remarry and I move to Tennessee. And if that isn't crazy enough, I told him that if he likes the property, to go ahead and buy it – sight unseen by me. There was a time when I would never have considered anything like this. It is a huge investment to make without seeing first, but that's what faith is all about.

If this farm turns out to be the one, we would close at the attorney's office by the end of August and I would put my house on the market here immediately afterward. Sandwiched in there somewhere would be a wedding and a notice of resignation for the bank. I really dread handing in that resignation. My career has been my lifeline for so many years. I think I will be lost without my job.

Dolly, I hope you don't think I have lost my mind, but this is the best chance I have to live with horses. Try to get some rest and I will talk to you soon. 'Night, Dolly

ଓଓଔ

ⓒ Before you buy, consider whether or not it makes sense to try to find an existing facility, or to build on vacant land. Generally, it is cheaper and easier to buy an existing farm than to build it from the ground up. But it may be difficult to find what you need in a property that someone else has owned. If the layout doesn't suit your needs, the costs involved in changing or adding on may be more than actually planning and building from your own plans.

ⓒ For instance, we purchased property with an existing pole shed and built a barn around it. This was a lot easier than trying to adapt a large barn for our horses. You can repair fencing, stalls, and roofs, but if the foundation and main supports of an existing structure are not sound, then you might as well start from the ground up and build it yourself.

ⓒ You'll want to make sure that the terrain offers proper drainage. If you don't have this, count on lots of mud in the paddocks and around the barn doors. In our situation, we had a lot of underground water that made the stalls soupy after a heavy rain. We installed drains around the barn and now use stall mats, which solved our problem.

ⓒ You want to look for rolling land, because it drains well and gives horses better exercise than flat land. Walk the land before you buy it to see where the water stands after a rain. Look for property that already has good pastureland and a natural water source. This way you don't have to run water lines to the pasture and seed the fields.

ⓒ Do you want to be close to town or totally isolated? Usually, land far away from the city is less expensive, so you may be able to have a larger property for your horses. Zoning probably won't be a problem, either. Your goal is to buy the best place you can afford for your horses; remember, it's a lifetime commitment.

Dear Dolly, Guess what? You already knew, didn't you? The sellers accepted our offer on the farm. It is a divorce situation and they are anxious to move, so we were able to negotiate a fair price. I'm excited and extremely nervous. All of a sudden this is really hitting me – I'm about to change my life completely. There is so much to think about. I haven't even considered how I am going to move two horses. As a good friend of mine used to say when she was faced with unpleasant decisions, "I'll worry about that another day."

ಬೊೀಆ

Dear Dolly, I know I haven't had much time to talk with you lately, but I can feel your presence. This weekend I went to Tennessee to close the deal on the farm. At the attorney's office, everyone asked me what I thought about the place. Imagine their surprise when I replied, "I haven't seen it yet, but I will after I leave here."

I finally did see the property and I loved it. It has a lot of open, green pasture with a pond and a slight hill for the horses to run back and forth. It is fenced, but it needs cross fencing. The house is ordinary, but the pole shed has real possibilities. We can't wait for the project of barn building to begin (or should I say Ron can't wait; I will be in Asheville selling my house and resigning from the bank).

On Sunday, Ron and I went to a pretty wedding chapel in town and remarried. The ceremony took all of five minutes, but I made him drive around the block a couple of times before we went in so that I could muster the courage to go through with it. Is that a warning sign, Dolly? The hard part came afterward. Ron's family came over to his brother's for dinner and we announced that we had remarried. They were all completely in shock and even though they were gracious, they know our history and think that we are totally out of our minds. It is perfectly understandable that they are worried about us – I'm worried about us, too! But his brother, brother-in-law and father all said they would be glad to help build the barn. The scary part is that this military/subdivision family has never been involved in building anything. It's a challenge and they are looking forward to the experience, but I think the novelty will surely wear off quickly.

We honeymooned at Wal-Mart, where I picked up a For Sale sign for my house in Asheville. Here I am at 2:00 a.m., writing a letter of resignation from the job I love. I had no idea that this would be so difficult. I will give thirty days' notice, making my last day October 15. I know it's no use going to bed, because I won't sleep until I get this over with. Stay right where you are, and if I need help I'll call you, okay? 'Night, Dolly

ೞCಛ

Dear Dolly, Just as I thought! The statement I made a while ago about selling my home immediately could not have been more accurate. I put a *For Sale* sign in my yard this morning before I went to work. I had four calls on my answering machine and a lady waiting outside my house when I arrived home this evening.

I had told my co-workers a little white lie in case someone who knew me called to inquire about the house. I said that I was going to put my house on the market and see what happened. I remarked that if it sold, I would then find a property with some acreage. It was actually a stall tactic, because if I wasn't able to sell for some reason, I wouldn't be able to move to Tennessee and I didn't want to be out of a job. For that reason, the letter of resignation was written but not delivered yet.

I called all the people who inquired about my house and have two appointments for Friday evening. The lady who was waiting outside my house lives down the street. She realized that the house was out of her price range, but she wondered if she could just look through it. This house is on the historic register and was completely renovated before I bought it. I gave my neighbor the grand tour and she was on her way. It gave me pause to think about what a truly beautiful house I am giving up. I hate to part with it, but my plans do not include living in a house in the city. My initial thought was to rent it, but the upkeep would be too much, so I will simply accept the best offer. 'Night, Dolly

ೞCಛ

Dear Dolly, I need legal advice! Not your field, huh? I received not one, but *two* offers on my house today. One is for full

51

cash price with some conditions and the other is for more than full cash price with no conditions. The first offer was presented by a young couple who are both lawyers and really want this house. The second offer is from a lady who grew up in Asheville and is now living in Colorado. She wants to move back and this house is perfect for her. After talking with a real estate attorney, I am inclined to accept her offer. We will finalize the transaction in thirty days. With the house under contract, the time has come to resign from the bank. I will do this tomorrow. I'll let you know what happens, as if you wouldn't already know anyway by simply eavesdropping.
'Night, Dolly

৪৩০৪

Dear Dolly, I sent copies of my letter of resignation to my regional president and gave the original to my manager. She was completely surprised by my resignation. She is an overachiever like myself, so I imagine she thinks I've lost my sanity. There was a time in my life when I would never have walked away from success and money. I never thought I would hear myself say, "It's different this time." I didn't tell my manager where I am going, but I did check the personnel manual and confirmed that an officer has to give thirty days' written notice. This will give me the time to continue working while I pack and wait for closing on the house.

Rather than have my co-workers find out from someone else that I had resigned, I told them as soon as I could after submitting the letter of resignation. I had to produce a copy of the resignation letter to convince them that it was true. "You're an institution," they all said. While I'm pleased with the compliment, I know they will carry on splendidly when I'm gone.

No one knew that I had remarried until today. Ron called and asked if he could speak with his wife. My administrative assistant asked him to repeat himself. He said, "This is Ron Bridges and I would like to speak with my wife." She couldn't believe it. They all think I have lost my ever-lovin' mind. At this point, no one has put two and two together and deduced that I am moving to Tennessee. I'm sure they will soon enough,

52

but a letter of resignation is cause for enough stress for one day. 'Night, Dolly

Ω℧

Dear Dolly, Well, the cat is out of the bag. The movers called me at work today and someone overheard. I confessed that I am moving to a farm that Ron and I have bought in Tennessee and that Maria and Lilli will follow in November. Everyone is excited for me, but as the days linger on, I'm beginning to feel totally detached from here. My days are numbered and I know that I am not effective at work, although I try to be. I've resigned from other positions before and I think it's funny how loyalty lies with the present. That always seems to be the case.

I am planning to close on this house and move on October 15th, my last day at the bank. Everything is ready, so pack your bags and be ready to fly, Dolly. Can you even fly over the mountains? Will you be happy in Tennessee? Your whole life was spent in North Carolina, as well as your afterlife. I could not face the move if I thought you would not come with me. Now that I've found you again you are such a big part of my life. Please tell me that it won't change anything between us, Dolly. You will always be my special horse. 'Night, Dolly

Ω℧

Dear Dolly, This is it! Moving day! The movers came yesterday, packed everything and drove through the night toward Tennessee. I ordered one last pizza from Pizza Hut (it was free because of all the business I have given them over the years) and slept in agony on the hardwood floors. Then I closed the deal at the attorney's office at 9:00 a.m. and drove by to look at the house one more time. Then I headed out.

It was a four-hour drive and I felt a tremendous gravity pulling me towards the mountains of Asheville as I drove toward Knoxville. Something kept calling me to come back. No matter where I may live in the future, I will never experience the contentment I enjoyed living in these beautiful western North Carolina Mountains. And I expect that every time I visit, I will have a gigantic lump in my throat.

53

As I drew closer to our new home, my excitement built. I exited the interstate about twenty miles east of Nashville and headed for the little town square. I turned north and drove about five miles until I saw the driveway of our new home. Then I spotted the moving van and in the distance, the biggest surprise of all. The barn! Over the past few weekends Ron and his family had worked diligently and there was an honest-to-goodness barn (though still very sketchy) taking shape! The horses will not arrive until November, so there will be plenty of time to work on it.

The new house is a lot smaller than my house in Asheville, but I keep reminding myself that I wanted land and a barn, not a house. My lifestyle is about to change, so I don't need a big house to keep up. It will be an easy house to maintain and it does have a full basement. Above all, the real emphasis here is on the horses.

Initially Ron and I were going to name the farm Second Chance (because we were given one), but our plan is to raise and sell Arabian horses. Who would want to purchase a horse that came from a farm called Second Chance? It sounds like a last-leg retirement home to me. So, after walking the property and feeling the breeze that seems to persist, we decided that the perfect name is Summerwind Farm.

The great challenge I have to face now is to see if you are here, Dolly. What if you couldn't get past the mountains? What if that was the pull I felt drawing me back? What will I do if you don't live at Summerwind?

Give me a sign, Dolly. If you're here, let me know somehow. In the meantime, I'll think about you really hard and wish for days long ago. 'Night, Dolly

ഇൻവ

Dear Dolly, On this peaceful night with no wind to stir the wind chimes, Ron and I sat on the front porch of our new home. Suddenly, a slight breeze stirred the chimes and they made the most beautiful music. That's when I knew that you had made the trip with me. You are going to share these beautiful green pastures with my other horses. Now I can call this home, Dolly, because you are here. Thank you. I can go forward now. Welcome home, Dolly

ഇരുങ്ങ

Dear Dolly, Now that we have made the move to the farm, Ron and I are working as much as we can to get the barn ready for Lilli and Maria. We work each night after he gets home from his "real" job, and on the weekends his father, brother and brother-in-law get together for mass construction. The barn is really taking shape and I can hardly wait to sleep in the barn and listen to the rain falling on the tin roof.

When Ron knew he was going to build a barn, he had a source for the wood he would need. The brick that is shipped to his company arrives on rail cars, and is braced by wooden bulkheads that are eight feet long. That wood happens to be solid oak and will be the perfect material for the inside of the barn. Each week, Ron hauls the pallets home, dismantles them and stacks them beside the barn.

While the barn will not be as large as we would like, we will have room for a box stall for Maria and a double foaling stall for Lilli. The foaling stall can be partitioned to make two stalls later. We also plan to have a tack and feed room and a small loft.

We have spent a lot of money on start-up supplies and tack. I had no idea that first aid supplies, fly sprays, grooming equipment and supplements could be so costly. I wouldn't have given much thought to the cost when I was employed, but I haven't looked for a job yet. I have to rely on Ron's income and the money I brought from my accounts in North Carolina. I hope I can wait until Lilli's foal is born before I have to return to work.

Dolly, wouldn't it be great if I could see the actual birth? This will be my first time, so I'm a little nervous about taking on such a big responsibility. However, everyone I know who is involved with horses says that the mare does all the work, and that the chances of seeing a birth are very slim. It would appear that somehow mares know how to outsmart humans and give birth secretly. We'll just see about that!

The barn is coming along nicely, and it should be ready by the end of November. I really want all the construction completed so that I can concentrate on the two mares. The fencing company has cross-fenced the pasture for us and built a round pen. I'm a little concerned about the round pen, as the ground is not terribly level. We were in a hurry to get things ready for the horses and I think we have made a big mistake. I'll have to ride Maria when she gets here and decide if the footing in the round pen is suitable. If not, to quote my friend in Asheville, "We'll worry about that another day".

The weather is really hot and humid, just like when we lived in Birmingham. You wouldn't know anything about that, living where you are, would you, Dolly? But each morning I get up and work around the barn, making sure that things are right, and by 11:00 a.m. I am exhausted because of the heat. Of course, I'm not the spring chicken I once was. Funny how I waited so long to get into something I loved. Live and learn takes on a whole new meaning, huh? 'Night, Dolly

೮೦೦೪

Dear Dolly, Boy, have our plans changed! Remember how I said that Lilli and Maria would be here by the end of November? Try the second week in November! Shelby called yesterday and said that she knew a hauler who had an opening at that time and that we should go ahead and move them. Although I am paying her for their training and board, I think she would rather I get them out of her hair. That surely puts the pot on the hot burner! We'll just have to crank up the construction workers and make sure the grill is fired up and ready to cook steaks as compensation.

Everything is almost ready, anyway. Ron did a great job on the inside of the barn using the oak. He also has enough left over if we decide to add on in the future. I have ordered shavings for the stalls to be delivered this morning, and Ron has arranged for hay to be delivered on the first rain-free day. Just to be safe, he is going to pick up a few bales to get us started. Wouldn't you know it? It has been totally dry until the horses are due to arrive, and now the rain starts and we have lots of mud around here. I guess that's true with any start-up operation, but it sure seems that we have more than our share. 'Night, Dolly

೮೦೦೪

The first year we were plagued by mud. More than once, I actually got my feet stuck in the mud and lost a shoe or two. Here are some things we did to help us get control and reduce the risk of injury to our horses:

- ೦೪ Keep water tanks away from the barn area so that the horses' traffic will not make existing mud worse, or create new mud.

- ೦೪ If you have a high pasture, utilize this for grazing until the barn area dries out.

- ೦೪ Install gutters or downspouts to divert water away from the barn.

57

- ⋐ Use small gravel to make a base around the highly-traveled areas of the barnyard. Plant grasses such as Bermuda on top of the gravel. Keep horses off the area until the grass has taken root.

- ⋐ Plant trees in areas that have a lot of water runoff, but be sure to fence around them to keep the horses away.

Dear Dolly, Well, today's the day the girls come to Tennessee. Shelby called at 6:00 a.m. to say that they both loaded beautifully and that in about eight hours I would see them again. I'm so excited! This is the life I've wanted for four years. I so look forward to waking up in the morning and walking out the back door, to be greeted by my own horses. This will be much better than going to the boarding stable to visit. Of course, I know that there will be a lot more work, but I'm kind of looking at that as therapy. It will be soothing to take care of the barn and the horses. The hay was delivered last night and the stalls are bedded with clean, fluffy shavings, so all I need now are two horses. Dolly, I'm going to go wait by the window and look down the driveway. Talk to you later.

༄༅

Dear Dolly, I see them – do you? They are riding in a big white trailer and they each have their own window. The trailer is pulling up to the barn. Gotta go!

Dolly, it was so neat. I had worked so long and hard to make sure that the stalls were just right for Lilli and Maria, and what was the first thing they did? Poop! Well, at least they feel right at home. I'm going to have the vet check them just to make sure that the pregnant one, Lilli, is okay after the long trip. The task at hand is to find a vet. I don't expect help from you on this, because I know you're new here, too. The Yellow Pages it is, then! 'Night, Dolly

༄༅

Chapter Six
The Orientation

Dear Dolly, Finding a vet is a lot harder than I thought. Most of the vets here prefer cattle to horses. There was only one who listed a large animal practice, so I called his office and he came out yesterday. I was riding Maria in the front yard when he and his assistant drove up. The first thing the vet did was to chastise me for riding in sneakers. I know that you are supposed to ride with shoes that have heels, but I was so anxious to ride Maria for the first time at Summerwind, I just grabbed my sneakers. The vet then went to great lengths to tell me how when he was a boy, his foot got caught in the stirrup because he had no heels on his shoe. He was dragged quite a way and suffered multiple injuries. So, that's the foot on which we got started (no pun intended).

Then the vet examined Lilli and everything checked out fine. He said that he would be happy to assist us when foaling time arrived, but he went on to say that to be perfectly honest, most births happened in the middle of the night when no one was around. He said we had virtually no chance of being witness to the event. Although his manner was very abrupt, I did like him.

Thank God for my trainer friend, Shelby. She has fielded a lot of calls from me with really stupid questions about horse care. But she takes it all in stride and everything she tells me I write down in a notebook. Hopefully, I won't ask the same question twice.

I was right about the round pen. I tried to work Maria in it this morning, and it is a long way from being level. Since it would take a lot of fill and work to level, I think we will move it to the front of the barn where it is naturally more level. The ideal spot is just where my father-in-law is planning to have a garden, but I don't have the heart to ask him to move the garden. I'll figure something out. 'Night, Dolly

ಬಂಡಿ

Dear Dolly, Well, the round pen has been re-built in the front of the barn, off to one side. We ordered some fill and it looks a lot better now. I have been riding Maria in the mornings to acquaint her with the round pen, but today I am back to my cold-natured self and am staying indoors. The weather has turned really cold here lately and it snowed last night. I know you felt that! Naturally, I would like to take electric blankets to the barn for Lilli and Maria (just kidding), but all of my books tell me that they are perfectly comfortable in this type of weather. Besides, you never had any of the frills, did you? The old barn had huge gaps between the boards, providing barely any shelter. But you were fine and lived to be 34. It just goes to show you.

I have been worried about riding the horses in the snow and ice with shoes on. I still think about that day we rode in Asheville when the horses slipped on the ice. That was very dangerous. Think safety. 'Night, Dolly

ಬಿ೦೮

Here are some things to remember about winterizing your horse:

- ೮೩ Horses can acclimatize to the cold, but need some sort of protection from the wet and wind, such as a run-in-shed.

- ೮೩ Horses that are pasture kept and are not worked daily will usually fare well without blanketing. In colder climates, however, it may be necessary to blanket the horse in order to maintain body heat.

- ೮೩ Watch for icy balls of snow that get stuck in a horse's shoes and remove them daily.

- ೮೩ When you groom the pasture-kept horse, be careful to brush snow off his coat and not down into it.

- ೮೩ Each horse has individual feeding requirements; keep a close watch for any signs of weight loss or other changes in body condition. This may be hard to detect if the horse has a thick winter coat. In extreme weather, increase the daily amount of high quality hay by 10 to 20 percent.

cʒ In the winter, an idle adult horse still needs a minimum of 10-12 gallons of water daily. Horses are more susceptible to colic in the winter months because their water intake decreases. It can be a real challenge to keep water tanks free of ice, but it is a necessary task to keep the horse drinking.

cʒ Provide a salt and trace mineral block in an accessible area out of the weather.

Dear Dolly, I think Ron is coming around to this horse stuff. I read every book or magazine article that I can get my hands on, and I pass it along to him. At first, he wouldn't even put halters on Lilli and Maria, but now he is taking the initiative. Ron has ridden both Lilli and Maria, but he isn't comfortable on them. A couple of times he came right off. I know the horses are just having fun with Ron and it is only his lack of riding experience that is the problem. He keeps asking for a "broken down old trail horse" of his own. Lilli is becoming very broad, as the foal is due around the middle of April. I think I will look around and see if I can find a seasoned horse for Ron to ride. I'm also going to mention this to Shelby to see if she can put the word out in North Carolina. 'Night, Dolly

ༀცঙ

Dear Dolly, Great news! It took a bit of searching, but Shelby called and told me about a bomb-proof horse that she has found for Ron. He is part mustang and part Belgian draft horse and weighs nearly 1300 pounds. His name is Jerry and he is accustomed to farm work. Jerry's "family" included two teenagers, who have now decided that they would rather have a four-wheeler than a horse. Sight unseen and taking Shelby's word on it, I told her to load Jerry up and bring him to Tennessee.

The agreement was for Shelby and her husband to deliver Jerry and the two-horse trailer we are buying from them on Saturday afternoon, a ten-hour trip. I can't even imagine my look when I saw that horse. Dolly, I thought you were big! To capture the moment, I took a picture of Ron's face when Jerry backed out of that trailer!

He is massive, with a beautiful sorrel coat and a flaxen mane and tail. Shelby's husband was clearly taken with Jerry and he remarked as we went to greet them, "Emily, if it had been anybody except you, they wouldn't have gotten Jerry away from us."

We took turns riding Jerry and it compared to sitting in an overstuffed easy chair. He even follows us around like I remember you doing, Dolly, without even a lead or halter. All you have to do is say, "Come on, Jerry," and he follows behind on the right side.

We put Jerry into a stall for the night, but we quickly realized that our stalls were not big enough for him and he was sure to become cast at some point. Besides, Shelby said that Jerry was accustomed to sleeping outside under the stars with a pasture full of cows keeping him company. Ron began working on a run-in shed the very next day, but even on the coldest of nights Jerry chose to lie flat out on the cold ground. Early one morning last week I went running to the pasture at breakneck speed to check on Jerry, because I thought he was dead. He wasn't dead; he picked his head up to look at me as I approached as if to say, "Don't sneak up on me like that, can't you see that I'm sleeping?"

Dolly, it's really nice to have a horse that Ron can ride with confidence. It has made all the difference in the world in his enthusiasm, which still measures a lot lower than mine. Ron really looks at this venture as a novelty and always tells everyone he meets that we're new at this. On the other hand, I wing it and pretend that I know what I'm doing.

We're in for an experience tonight, Dolly. The vet is coming out to give Jerry a checkup and his vaccinations. Aren't you glad you don't have to have shots anymore? Life must be very easy up there. 'Night, Dolly

ങ്ങരു

Dear Dolly, The first few weeks that Jerry lived at Summerwind, he was a model horse, but now, as the newness wears off, he is beginning to show signs of the *real* Jerry. Even though he will respond to leg cues, he has never had

62

instruction on head set or rein cues. Jerry is a workhorse, so I have started to re-educate myself. I suppose he was trained about the same way that you were. "Go" works well and "whoa", "trot" and "canter" are okay. Jerry will *not* respond to rein pressure. At times I have to pull with all my strength just to get him turned around. Now bear in mind that he only behaves this way when he leaves the barn, not on the return trip. Jerry is more than happy to trot back in that direction. So I spend lots of time working on the barn sour routine.

Ron rides Jerry more than I do, because he says that Jerry is a real horse, not one of "those Arabs." We have been taking Jerry and Maria on the trails near our house. One day, we had come back from a ride and I decided to canter Maria along the side of the yard, leaving Ron and Jerry behind. As I walked Maria toward the orchard, I heard Ron yelling at the top of his lungs. I turned Maria toward the noise, only to see Jerry – alone – hauling himself to the barn at a gallop that would invoke jealousy from the Thoroughbreds at Churchill Downs. Maria looked back at me as if to say, "Should I follow him or what?" But she stood steady and shortly Ron dusted himself off and trotted up the driveway.

When he got to the barn, Ron mounted Jerry and rode him back down to the front of the yard. Then he started walking Jerry back to the barn, hoping to teach him to proceed slowly. Jerry missed the point of the lesson and began galloping to the barn again. However, this time Ron held on and rode him. He turned Jerry around and repeated the lesson. Jerry began to catch on, or maybe he was just tired, because the next time he trotted to the barn and the time after that he walked back like a proper horse.

One weekend, Ron and I loaded Jerry and Maria into the trailer for a highly anticipated trail ride at a park near Nashville. We had waited a long time to take this ride, but our excitement was interrupted when a sudden thunderstorm brought a downburst of rain. Although we were able to wait out the rain in the thick forest, Maria was very agitated and we thought it best to head back to the stable. We untacked the horses, loaded Jerry and started to load Maria. She immediately started to back up. We tried several times to get her to move forward, but she planted her feet and refused to budge. I have read plenty about proper loading techniques, but I have only loaded horses that are well trained, and Maria is (usually) one of them. That's why she caught me completely off guard. I couldn't understand why she was acting this way, unless she was upset by the passing thunderstorm. The crisis at hand was getting Maria home, and despite repeated attempts, Ron and I could not get her into the trailer.

Thankfully, two other couples saw our dilemma and asked if they could help. One lady went to get sweet feed, saying that it always worked. It didn't work this time. Maria was planted firmly in one spot. Finally, after struggling for another thirty minutes, it took all six of us pulling together on a long lead rope behind Maria's hindquarters until little by little, she stepped into the trailer. Thank goodness there are people who will help others in a bind. I'm very grateful to them for helping or we might still be there. 'Night, Dolly

ⓘ

- ☙ A barn sour horse is fighting for control and needs to be worked daily away from the barn. Whenever he turns toward the barn, reverse him and continue working him away for a while longer. It may take a long time to get back to the barn, but this is necessary in order for you to establish control.

- ☙ Sometimes the horse won't move beyond a certain point on the trail. If this happens, turn the horse around in a small circle and try again. Be consistent and persistent, and when the horse decides to move forward, reward him. This may take a while, too.

- ☙ Horses like to anticipate your moves, so be ready. The minute you think that the horse is getting ready to do something on his own, correct him before he makes his move. Once again, you control what the horse does.

- ☙ If at any time you feel that you have lost control, return to an area of training that you were in complete control. Begin working from this point for a solution to the problem.

Dear Dolly, The last few weeks assure me that you are watching over me. Ron and I took a much- needed break from the horses and went out to a Mexican restaurant one Friday evening for dinner. On Saturday, I didn't feel very well, but it wasn't serious enough to hinder my riding or working at the barn. Then on Sunday, I began to feel very uncomfortable and had a lot of pain in my upper right side. Thinking it was a reaction to the meal on Friday, I ignored the pain and continued to work in my flower garden. Around 1:00 p.m. I finally suggested to Ron that I go to the emergency room. Now, Dolly, you know how difficult it is for me to admit that. I am not one to go to the doctor, so you know I was in excruciating pain.

I waited at the hospital for two hours before anyone could see me. Then a doctor examined me, said that it sounded like a gall bladder attack and called in a surgeon to examine me. All I could think about were the horses and their well being. Who would take care of them? Up to this point I had done all the feeding and Ron didn't even know what the horses ate.

The surgeon finally arrived and after examining me, decided that the diagnosis was inconclusive and that he needed to admit me for tests. I asked him to give me something for the pain and let me go home. I promised to return the next morning, but the doctor wisely said no to that idea. I was so sick that even the prospect of Ron feeding the horses didn't bother me.

The entire day on Monday was taken up with tests of all sorts, and finally around 7:00 p.m. the doctor came into my room. He thought the culprit was my gall bladder, but wasn't completely sure. Anyway, he said, it needed to come out. I was rushed to the operating room just as Ron came back from feeding the horses. The last thing I said to him was, "Take care of the horses."

The surgeon removed the gall bladder by laparascopic surgery and called my husband from the operating room to say that it didn't look that bad. He decided to explore some more and thank God he did, or I wouldn't be here at Summerwind now.

It seems that my appendix had relocated itself behind my colon and couldn't easily be detected by the camera. It had ruptured and if the surgeon had waited much longer, the prognosis would have been very different. That surgery was by incision, so I now have a series of scars to brag about.

Dolly, I hope you missed me because I missed you. I had to stay in the hospital for a week and I can't ride for another six weeks. Ron's dad is going to help with the barn chores and if I know him, he will make very sure that I don't venture out of the house. That's okay; he can't be here all of the time and I need to see my horses. Tonight I get to sleep in my own bed again. It's so good to be home. 'Night, Dolly

ഇൻൻ

Dear Dolly, I must have had part of my brain removed while I was in the hospital. But I decided to take the round pen down and build an arena. I reasoned that the round pen hadn't been that functional and that an arena would give us more room to ride. And we could always close off part of the arena to make a round pen when we needed it. The good news is that Ron agreed.

After getting two estimates from fencing companies, Ron concluded that he could do the work himself and save a fair amount of money. He could use the boards that are around the existing pen and buy others to match them. This time, however, we asked a grading contractor to come out and look at the area and give us an estimate on the leveling. He was very fair in his bid and we liked him right away. He is going to start next week. I'll keep you posted. 'Night, Dolly

ഇൻൻ

Dear Dolly, With those big ears I know you heard my praise for Ron when the arena was completed. He did a great job with the rails and we ordered sand for the footing. It was delivered this morning, so I should actually be able to ride tomorrow. The footing in the round pen was much too hard for the horses. I have heard that this could cause shock to their feet. See, I'm learning as I go. 'Night, Dolly

ഇൻൻ

Dear Dolly, It took a long time for me to get my energy back after my operation, but I slowly returned to my old cantankerous self. Both Ron and I rode Jerry off and on through the winter, but as Ron's work schedule became more demanding and my time was spent with the other horses, Jerry stood idle in the pasture more often than not. Since he had spent his entire life working and being useful, the leisure time began to take a toll on him. He started to kick out at the other horses and wouldn't let them drink from the pasture water tank. Jerry's favorite pastime became constantly clanging on the metal gate. Jerry has huge draft horse feet, so his shoes caused terrible damage to the gate. Jerry was so smart that the minute I opened the back door, some six hundred feet away, he heard me and ran away from the gate. Then when I closed the door, he started all over again.

After having to buy two replacement gates, Ron and I sat down to discuss the feasibility of Jerry remaining on the farm. Yes, he had helped Ron learn to stay on a horse, but no, he was not a happy camper and took it out on everyone else. I loved to ride Jerry, but I didn't have time to work with him. Also, Ron worked a heavy schedule and his spare time was taken up with farm chores that I couldn't physically perform. Reluctantly, we made the decision to sell Jerry to a good home.

I posted ads at the Co-op, tractor supply and feed stores and ran an ad in the newspaper. Nothing happened for three weeks. I was beginning to have seller's remorse when a call came in from a man who lived very close to us. He asked if we still had the horse, and I said that we did. He and his wife came out that very day to meet Jerry and liked what they saw. They told us that they would talk it over and get back to us.

They owned a property similar to ours, but they owned cows and one Appaloosa mare. They wanted a companion for her and a horse for the trail occasionally. If Jerry had it easy at our house, he surely would have it much easier there. And instead of three horses with one on the way, there would be only two, therefore allowing more time for one-on-one with Jerry.

A week went by before we heard from them again. By this time, we had made a video to send to our friend in North Carolina who knew someone interested in Jerry. But UPS lost the video and by the time it showed up, the first couple had called to say that Jerry would be the perfect addition to their family. They did, however, want to ride him first.

When they arrived, I was riding Jerry in the arena, but the man asked if he could use his own saddle. He mounted Jerry and started riding, and I knew from the glimmer in his eyes that Jerry's sale was a done deal. A little tug at my heartstrings made me want to reconsider, but I knew that Jerry needed more than we could give him. And we certainly couldn't afford to keep replacing gates!

The transaction was made, a check was in hand and they asked us to deliver Jerry the next afternoon. At that time, I had a Jeep Cherokee and I was a little concerned about pulling Jerry with it. We had used the Jeep to haul our Arabians, but they were considerably lighter. To add to my concern, the new owners lived at the top of a very steep hill. I was a little nervous on the way over, but even more nervous when I saw that driveway. But the Jeep rose to the task at hand and we safely rounded the hill. We unloaded Jerry and took him into the barn where the Appaloosa mare named Princess waited for her new stablemate. Jerry was led straight to a stall where alfalfa hay was waiting, and I knew that he was going to be fine. We told him good-bye and left, and I must say that I felt a burden lift.

Jerry was a horse that needed to work, and we had placed him in the wrong environment. I think humans expect too much of horses sometimes, don't you, Dolly? It is unfair to think that radical changes can be imposed on horses without mostly negative consequences. I like to think that we corrected this injustice to Jerry and I'm not afraid to admit that I made a mistake. I know that Jerry is happy now, because he is in a home with fewer horses and has more attention. It's the right fit for Jerry and that's what I wanted for him.
'Night, Dolly   ଞୈଓ

Chapter Seven
Lilli's Baby And A Mysterious Illness

Dear Dolly, I am getting so excited about Lilli's baby. We have begun to get her stall ready, changing the shavings to wheat straw for bedding and getting the necessary items ready for the birth. We have also viewed the tape "Foaling Fundamentals" umpteen times. Neither of us knows anything about foaling, so we are trying to cover all the bases. Even though Lilli has had other babies, this will be our first. Understandably, we are a little scared, but the excitement and the anticipation have overtaken our fright.

I hope you don't mind sleeping over the barn, Dolly, because our foaling vigil has begun. It is now April 10th, and aside from groaning when she lies down and pinning her ears every time we go to check on her, Lilli acts as though this is no big deal. So now we wait. 'Night, Dolly

ഇ�️ഗ

Dear Dolly, I guess you witnessed everything from above, but I became a horse grandmother today! After keeping foal watch for nine days, fatigue had begun to set in and Ron and I were at each other's throats. But contrary to what the vet said, this baby was born in broad daylight. And guess what, Dolly? I saw it all as it happened and lived to tell about it. Let me share our joy with you and tell you the whole story:

Today is April 20th and it was a beautiful Sunday morning. I decided to turn Lilli out in the corral near the barn while I gave her stall a thorough cleaning. I had taken her off pasture ninety days prior to this, because fescue is prevalent in this area. I always made sure that I gave Lilli plenty of grass and alfalfa hay. This morning was no different; but instead of chomping away as she usually did, she was extremely agitated. She ran around and around, gazing at the other horses in the pasture. I continued cleaning and constantly checked on Lilli, but she did not calm down. I gave her fresh water and brought carrots to her at noon. She was sweating on her shoulders by this time, but the day was warm and she was in the sun. The day crept by.

Ron and his father were in the upper pasture cross-fencing a new section for grazing. At 5:30 p.m. I brought the horses in for feeding. Lilli was the last in, and as usual I wrapped her tail for the evening before putting her in her stall. As I bent over to grasp her tail, I noticed the unmistakable droplets of milk on her teats. She was sweating all over her shoulders and flanks. I called for Ron, but he was unable to hear me. I knew that Lilli's baby was coming, but I still believed we had lots of time.

I started to lead Lilli toward her stall, and her water broke while we were still standing in the hallway of the barn. She looked at me with wide eyes as though to say, "Oh, no! What do I do now?" I looked at her the very same way. I managed to get her into the stall by letting her take little stutter steps, then I ran partway up the hill and yelled at the top of my lungs "Lilli's in labor! Come now!" At first Ron didn't get what I was saying, but all of a sudden he looked like sparks had ignited around him and he and his dad got into the truck and sped toward the barn.

I hurried back into the barn and found Lilli lying down and two tiny feet already out. I checked to make certain that the feet were pointed downward and they were. I breathed a little easier as I waited for Ron. I cautioned Ron to slow down as he came barreling into the barn, and we both froze in space to let Lilli have privacy in this most sacred time. The birth process took only a few moments and was completely textbook. I asked Ron to slip into the stall behind Lilli in case the baby could not free itself from the sac, while I ran to call the vet. We were both so excited that it seemed everything moved in slow motion.

When I got back to the stall, the foal was sitting up in a daze and was the most beautiful little filly I had ever seen. (Naturally!) We came completely unglued at that point and started ranting and raving and oohing and aahing, doing all the things we should not have done. For instance, I knew that peace and quiet is very important, but after all, it was our first baby! To top it all off, Ron's dad had now arrived in the barn, so the three of us stood there, chatting away and leaning over the stall door. But Lilli took it all in stride and was a perfect mother from the outset. She didn't even pin her ears at me once.

After we recovered from the initial shock of seeing the actual birth, Ron gave the little filly a closer look. Suddenly he exclaimed, "Emily! Her feet are deformed!" Panic set in as he pointed out the fleshy pads that covered each tiny foot. Then Ron's dad explained that the feet were perfectly normal and that the pads were there to protect the mother from kicks while the foal was inside the womb. He said that as soon as the filly began to walk, the pads would conform to her feet. Boy, was I relieved to learn that the filly wouldn't have to have corrective foot surgery!

The filly was a beautiful bay with a white blaze that covered the front of her face. She was very alert and was on her feet within thirty-five minutes of birth. With a little steadying, she was able to nurse soon after standing. From that point on, she did not stop. She would run and run and even broke into a canter. Then she would get tired, fall down and nap for a short time. Then she would run and run again. She had so much energy after being cooped up, and she was not going to be still ever again. We will probably laugh for a long time to come when we hear the familiar sound of her stomping, and it gives us joy to think about it. The vet I had paged called and said that he would be out first thing in the morning. We began the imprint process when the filly was two hours old.

We'll take a break, Dolly, and you can have some heavenly grass. I am going to get some well-deserved sleep. See you in the morning and I will tell you more about the little filly and the imprinting. 'Night, Dolly

80CB

We were fortunate that Lilli's labor and delivery went so smoothly. The following tips will help you understand the stages of labor and delivery and the signs to look for:

- ∞ While the mare is in the first stage of labor, she will become agitated and restless, and may paw at the floor or pace in her stall. She may even lie down and get back up several times. Sometimes the mare may act colicky and kick at her abdomen.

- ∞ Occasionally a mare can omit the first stage of labor and the first sign of imminent foaling is when the water breaks. When this happens, expect the foal to be delivered shortly.

- ∞ The second stage of labor is the actual birthing process and will normally last from ten to forty minutes. The mare usually lies down on her side, but she can deliver quite safely while standing. The risk to the foal in this situation is that the mare might position herself so that the foal drops against the wall, or she could step on it.

- ∞ The foal's feet should appear first and should be pointed downward. The mare may take a series of short rests after the head is out, but she usually takes a longer rest after the hips are delivered. However, some mares stand up immediately after the hips are delivered. When this happens, the umbilical cord breaks and the foal is on its own.

- ∞ The placenta is expelled within one to three hours of foaling. Without pulling on the placenta, tie it up as it is expelled so that it doesn't get stepped on. It is very important that the entire placenta be expelled from the mare in order for her reproductive tract to remain clear and less likely to become seriously infected. Your veterinarian will want to examine the placenta to make certain that it is intact.

Dear Dolly, Are you rested and ready to hear about the imprinting? I heard about this while I was at Shelby's barn in North Carolina. The purpose of imprinting is to create a bond between the foal and the imprint trainer. Such a thing didn't exist, to my knowledge, when you and I were young. But here goes, and it is a wonderful thing.

I first witnessed the imprinting process following the birth of a filly at Shelby's farm. The veterinarian who invented the technique, Dr. Robert Miller, has had much success with imprinting newborn foals. I purchased his video and familiarized myself with his technique. Naturally, I wanted our new baby to benefit from his methods, so I'll tell you what we did to the little filly last night.

While I stood beside Lilli, Ron began to rub the filly all over her body, carefully tapping her feet to simulate a farrier's touch and desensitizing any area of her body that would come in contact with human hands in the future. He also crackled plastic over her body, ran electric clippers around her (without blades) and sprayed a water bottle over her to simulate fly spray or spray medications. All this was done while he cradled her head in the backward position that she had been in while she was in Lilli's uterus. It was amazing to see how calm the filly was, and she flinched only a few times with each new procedure. The whole process took about an hour, and we repeated it again first thing this morning while we waited for the vet. We had made up our minds to do everything gently and calmly and we hoped that it would result in the baby being calmer, too. 'Night, Dolly

೩೦೦೩

Dear Dolly, The same vet who chastised me for wearing sneakers is the one who came today to check Lilli and the baby. I immediately became apprehensive, because I know that his area of expertise is cows instead of horses. But there were no equine vets in town and he was quick to respond. The minute he stepped into the barn, he became aggressive in his handling. He walked into the stall and started chasing the little filly, which upset Lilli, not to mention me. Then he wrestled the filly into a corner and gave her a shot. In the process of doing this he cut his hand and the filly got a cut above her eye. What a way to welcome her to the world of humans, huh?

The vet then proceeded to lecture me on the importance of teaching her to stand tied. We are talking about a filly not even eighteen hours old. He said that the best way to teach a foal to tie was to just tie it up and wait it out; there was a chance it might break its neck, but you had to establish control immediately. We thanked him, paid the bill and vowed never to call him again. Don't you agree, Dolly? All of the work we had done to ensure that this little filly entered a gentle world had gone out the window. How could she trust humans if they all acted this way?

This day has created a lot of stress. I hope that we can find a good vet who is kinder to the horses. I don't see the need for undue aggressiveness, Dolly. Let's sleep on it, okay? 'Night, Dolly

ଞଓଔ

Dear Dolly, I feel so good that I just had to share this with you. Pretend you weren't watching! It's so hard to surprise an angel. I started teaching the filly to lead today. She started wearing a halter at two days of age, so I just took a lightweight lead rope and cut it to about a 14" length. I fastened this on the filly's halter, and as she walked around in the stall, I would grab hold and walk along with her. She caught on easily, and soon she would lead anywhere I wanted her to go. She stops, turns and backs when I do, so we are on the right road to leading.

To tie her, Ron took a rope and draped it over a beam in the hallway of the barn. I took Lilli into the hallway and the filly naturally followed. While the rope was not secured, it provided resistance when the filly tried to follow her mother. The first time, she pulled back when she felt the resistance and Ron loosened the rope. The next time she walked forward, releasing the tension. After about ten minutes, she would stand still without trying to follow her mother. I was very proud of her.

I'm sorry that I didn't ask your opinion on the filly's name, Dolly, but I chose it when she was conceived. Her name is Diamahn 'Lil. And today Diamahn 'Lil took her first walk outdoors to meet the other horses. She was a little scared at first, but Lilli let her know that everyone was friendly and soon she was back to her regular routine of nursing, pooping and napping.

The three black Tennessee Walking Horses next door came to the fence and stood for a long time to reverently welcome Diamahn 'Lil to the world. They actually think they belong at Summerwind and are only separated by a fence. They hope that I will feed them whenever our horses are fed – and they are not usually disappointed.

Lilli is an excellent mother and it is amazing to watch her teach her baby the rules of pasture living. At the present time they are separated from the other horses, but Lilli will allow Diamahn 'Lil to make nose contact across the fence. Diamahn 'Lil is starting to "play graze", as I call it. She puts her head down, but so far she hasn't come up with any grass. Each day is a learning experience for Diamahn 'Lil – and for me. She is really growing and I can see changes in her daily. I love to grab a chair and watch Diamahn 'Lil as she gets acquainted with her surroundings.

We have taught Diamahn 'Lil to stand tied outside now and I have ponied her with Lilli. She does really well. I have tried to get Ron to hitch the trailer to the truck so that we can get them both loaded while Diamahn 'Lil is still small enough to handle easily, but so far he has avoided that one. I have read that it is very important to teach foals to load into the trailer when they are very young. I guess I'll just have to keep working on Ron. That's all the news for now. 'Night, Dolly

಼ೲೞ

Foals load best on trailers when they are very young and will follow their mother anywhere. Of course, the mother needs to be easy to load. Here are a few tips:

     ೞ The trailer should be backed into a depression, such as a ditch. This will create less of a step-up for mother and foal. Even if you have a trailer with a ramp, it is still wise to teach the foal to load into a step-up trailer. Remove the center partition, or swing it to one side.

- ಣ Lead the mother into the trailer and allow the foal to follow her. The foal will usually follow his mother without hesitation. The mare is the foal's security blanket and he needs her. If for some reason the foal doesn't follow his mother, give him a nudge forward on his hindquarters. A butt rope can also be used, but you will need another person to help you.

- ಣ Unload the same way and the foal will follow his mother.

- ಣ After you have loaded and unloaded several times in this manner, move the trailer to more level ground to allow for more of a step-up.

Dear Dolly, Today was Diamahn 'Lil's first outing into the "big pasture" to meet the other horses. I worried constantly, but I didn't need to. Lilli took on a whole new personality when she stepped out with her filly. No one is allowed to touch that baby! Lilli has a definite comfort zone, and when Diamahn 'Lil ventures out of it, Lilli immediately tells her to come back. It is so much fun to watch how the other horses respect her right to privacy. Diamahn 'Lil has already learned that she can nurse and nap in the big pasture and that she has lots of bodyguards.

I had a painful learning experience this morning. I had tied Lilli for grooming and Diamahn 'Lil was standing beside her, observing. Without thinking, I set the grooming box down in the center of the aisle. Diamahn 'Lil decided to investigate, stepped on the box, spooked and took off running like a rabbit, charging into me in the process. I fell backward and banged my head on the stall door. For an instant, I thought I was going to black out, but I managed to gather my wits off the floor.

Although I was very pleased to have the oak wood for the walls of the barn, now I know why it is called *hard*wood. I wasn't seriously injured, but it might have been a different story if Diamahn 'Lil was bigger. The moral of the story is to always place grooming boxes out of the reach of horses.
'Night, Dolly

৪০৫১

Dear Dolly, Yesterday I noticed Lilli standing at the gate of the small paddock, staring into the distance and not grazing. I thought maybe she missed being with her pasture mates, so I put her and Diamahn 'Lil into the bigger pasture. About thirty minutes later, I noticed Lilli lying down, with the filly prancing around her. At that point, I knew that something was wrong. Lilli never lay down in the pasture, and Diamahn 'Lil was becoming more upset by the minute. I brought them back to the small paddock, where Lilli immediately went down, sweating on her flanks. I called a local vet who came out within the hour. He checked Lilli and asked matter-of-factly, "Didn't we have rain earlier in the week? I'll bet you she has green grass colic. I'll tube her, give her some Banamine and she'll be just fine."

77

The vet informed me that he was going out of town, and he gave me the names of three other vets in case Lilli didn't get better. She did seem to improve and was grazing a little by the end of the day. At the vet's direction, I didn't give her any grain that night, but she ate the grass hay I gave her. Diamahn 'Lil did not seem fazed by all the commotion, because her mother was now upright and she could nurse. Ron and I slept at the barn last night, more for our peace of mind than for Lilli.

This morning, Lilli's appetite returned (I still withheld grain) and I put her into the small paddock with grass hay. She ate all of the hay, assisted by Diamahn 'Lil, but around 10 o'clock I noticed that she had diarrhea. I took her temperature and it was normal. Her gums were pink, but her breathing was more rapid than usual.

One of the names the vet had given me was an equine practitioner who lives about thirty minutes away. We had heard his name before and knew that he was always in demand. I suspected that it would be next to impossible to get him to come out in the middle of the day for a new patient, but I was really becoming concerned about Lilli. I made the call to his office and his wife answered. I introduced myself and told her that I had been referred. I could tell by the tone of her voice that I had reached a caring, dedicated person. She said that she would page the vet and have him call me. When he heard Lilli's symptoms, he agreed to make room for me. He said that he was certain his other patients would want him to do the same if it was their horse in distress.

The vet took one look at Lilli and told me that we indeed had a very sick horse. She had no fever, but by this time she was badly dehydrated. He immediately started an IV and antibiotics. He also took blood samples and said that he would call me with the results as soon as possible.

If you don't mind, stay here with me tonight. I can use your support, because I'm really worried about Lilli. I'm going to sleep next to her again tonight. 'Night, Dolly

ഇൻരു

Dear Dolly, This morning the vet called to ask about Lilli's condition. I told him that she was not eating or drinking, but that her temperature was normal. He said that he would be right out to check her. He gave her another IV and checked her other vital signs. Her gums were pale now and had a bluish cast to them. Lilli just stood with her head down, as though she were in a trance, while Diamahn 'Lil danced around her, oblivious to what was going on with her mother.

This afternoon, the vet came back and said that Lilli definitely needed one-on-one attention. While it was possible for him to keep Lilli hydrated while he waited on the results of the blood tests, he felt that Lilli needed to be in a 24-hour care facility. The vet advised that the University of Tennessee at Knoxville had an excellent teaching hospital, and that he would be glad to refer us. We were overwhelmed with this news, but we knew that we had to try to save Lilli if we could. She was growing weaker and nothing seemed to be turning her around. This was clearly the only option.

The vet made a call to the head of the teaching hospital, who advised that they had room for Lilli. After Ron called his dad to ask him to make the journey with him, he began to get the trailer ready for the four-hour trip. The last thing the vet said to me was, "Don't worry about hay or water or anything else, just get her there." At that point, it really sunk in that we were in trouble.

All of a sudden it hit me – what would we do with Diamahn 'Lil? It made no sense for a four-month-old filly to make the trip with an ailing mother, and Lilli certainly had enough to deal with without a baby to worry about. Wouldn't this be the perfect time to wean?

Ron backed the trailer up to the barn and I led Lilli out. She was very weak and loaded easily. I think Lilli knew that she needed help and that we were trying to give it to her. Although Diamahn 'Lil called out for her as she left, Lilli did not look back once. Under ordinary circumstances, she would have resisted any attempt to separate her from her baby. The trailer pulled out, and I could do nothing except wait.

Surprisingly, Diamahn 'Lil accepted her mother's absence after calling for her a few times. Maria immediately stepped in as surrogate mother. She seemed to know instinctively that Diamahn 'Lil needed someone to substitute, so she did just that. (Except for the nursing!) It was amazing to watch how another horse will suddenly become protective of a foal. Diamahn 'Lil still spent the first few hours walking up and down the path to the pasture in search of Lilli.

The trip with Lilli was uneventful, especially good news since Ron had not trailered a horse by himself before. When they arrived at the medical university, a team of doctors and students greeted them. Lilli was taken to an examination room and the doctors commented that she looked a lot better than they had expected after the conversation with the vet. They told Ron to go home and that they would call the next day.

Following today's events, I am a nervous wreck. I knew in my heart that Lilli was seriously ill, but I didn't expect this. Let's try to get some rest. I think I'm going to need my strength. 'Night, Dolly

଼ଠଔଔ

Dear Dolly, I'm guilty of not talking with you lately, but I have been trying to keep a positive attitude and it's taking all my energy. Anyway, I want to bring you up to speed on what's been going on with Lilli over the past few days.

A doctor called each morning with a progress report on Lilli, but so far, no firm diagnosis. The doctors were baffled by the combination of symptoms and were having difficulty reaching a conclusion. I consulted my medical books for information about equine illnesses and decided that Lilli either had salmonella or Potomac Horse Fever. One local vet even accused me of reading too much, so I thought it was best to wait for a diagnosis.

After four days, the vet who was responsible for treating Lilli called with a firm diagnosis: Potomac Horse Fever! Now that the disease had a name, they could begin aggressive treatment. One problem that had surfaced was that Lilli had lost much of her stomach lining. The doctor advised that the best way to try to rebuild it was with plasma. This treatment was very costly, but it had good results. Lilli had lost a lot of weight and still had diarrhea. But now we knew what we were fighting, at least.

At the end of six days, the doctor said that the diarrhea was beginning to check itself, and if she could get it under control, Lilli could be released. I was encouraged by that news, although the doctor still cautioned that we were not out of the woods yet. Finally, at the end of eight days, the long-awaited call came: we could bring Lilli home!

This morning, Ron and I made the trip to Knoxville in record time. Our first stop was at the business office, where I presented the insurance information to the nurse. She told me that it was customary for the bill to be paid by the horse's owner and reimbursed by the insurance company. The expense was unexpected, but one that we gladly paid. Then we rushed to see our girl.

When I walked toward Lilli's stall, I didn't recognize her. If it weren't for the halter she was wearing, I would have thought she was someone else's horse. Lilli had lost 100 pounds and her eyes were sunken. Where Lilli's bay coat had normally been shiny, it was now dull and patchy. She had a huge edema on her belly that was caused by the amount of fluids that were needed to keep Lilli's protein level stable. But when I called her name and she completely ignored me, I knew she was on the road to recovery!

We brought Lilli home amid the whinnies of welcome from Maria and the baby she left behind. Diamahn 'Lil was especially excited to show her mother that she was a big girl now. While Lilli was in the hospital, we had altered the birthing stall to make it into two stalls. I think this will work very well for Lilli and Diamahn 'Lil; they will be next to one another, but they won't be able to touch noses. Besides, Lilli is still too weak to care about the filly next door. The important thing is that Diamahn 'Lil was weaned, although I wouldn't recommend this particular method to anyone.

I'm really grateful to the doctors at the University of Tennessee for making Lilli well, but I'm beyond words of gratitude to the vet who referred us. I hope that he will be the horses' friend for many years to come. But for now, I'm going to say a special prayer for the beautiful horse in the barn and hope for a speedy recovery. 'Night, Dolly

ಬಿಯ

Dear Dolly, It's been loads of fun around here. For the next week after Lilli returned home, we had to give her coated aspirin and antibiotic pills daily. It was a continuous game to try to disguise the medicine, and Lilli usually won that game! I tried putting the pills in apples, carrots and sweet feed; Lilli picked the pills out every time. I finally crushed the pills and put them in applesauce and she gobbled it right up. We also had to apply nitroglycerine patches to her legs daily in an effort to prevent laminitis. We checked her feet constantly for swelling or heat. The vet had advised us early on that laminitis is a major concern with Potomac Horse Fever – and of course, I read lots of articles about it.

Now I am gradually getting Lilli back to the pasture. Her stomach had been robbed of "good" bacteria, something the doctors call *flora.* So she will run the risk of stomach ulcers until she is back to normal. But she is making steady progress and the vet says that I will be able to ride Lilli in another two weeks.

Potomac Horse Fever is not common to Tennessee; that is why the diagnosis seemed so remote and out of place. But we're going to have the horses vaccinated against it now. I know that this won't guarantee that a horse will remain free from the disease, but it will give us some peace of mind.
'Night, Dolly

ಬಿಯ

      ಡ Potomac Horse Fever (PHF) is a rickettsial disease transmitted by biting flies or mosquitoes. The disease was first detected along the Potomac River in Virginia and Maryland, but it now occurs in other states, including Tennessee. It is a very difficult disease to diagnose, as it carries many of the same symptoms as other infections. The disease is fatal in about 30 percent of cases.

☙ I had a shock when I filed the claim on Lilli's illness. First of all, I hadn't read the policy to begin with. If I had, I would have seen that Lilli had colic surgery insurance only, not medical insurance. There is a distinct difference and this mistake on my part was very costly.

☙ Secondly, the claim must be filed within 24 hours under most circumstances, something that I didn't do.

Dear Dolly, Just when I thought things were getting back to normal with Lilli since her illness, I tried to ride her for the first time. The round pen work, as always, went very well. But as I mounted her, she started to step with agitation, her head close to the ground. This was definitely not typical of Lilli. I continued to walk her, but she would walk a few steps and break into a trot. At the trot, she was fine for a few strides, and then she would stutter kick with her hind leg. This completely baffled me, so I decided that she must have some remaining problem stemming from the nitro glycerin patches. I called the vet and he is going to check her next week. My feet hurt. 'Night, Dolly

❧☙

Dear Dolly, The vet made a routine call on Lilli yesterday and while he was here, he checked her legs for problems. He did a lameness check by holding up her leg for 30 seconds, and when he released it he asked me trot her away from him. While the vet saw some hesitation in the movement of the leg that caused her trouble last week, he didn't think it was indicative of arthritis. Just to be safe though, he suggested x-rays of her legs. The x-rays showed minor arthritis in both her hind legs. He gave her a shot to lubricate her joints, and after four months we should be able to tell if there was any improvement. He advised that I should ride her routinely and continue to assess her.

I just want to know if you were up there watching when I rode Lilli today? She was her old self again and was perfect when I rode her in the arena. She really paid attention to me the way she did when we began our partnership in North Carolina. She listened to every leg command and made her turns beautifully. I think we are on the right path again and I feel encouraged. Hold that thought, Dolly.

A funny thing happened this afternoon. Lilli has become the self-appointed keeper of the barn. Ron was working on the stall doors, and at feeding time Lilli came in first to make sure that everything was okay. She inspected the doors and then snorted and entered her stall. Then the others followed suit. How funny! This behavior kind of surprises me, because Maria is the alpha mare. I guess she doesn't have any concerns where barn building is concerned, huh? Maybe she delegated that responsibility to Lilli. All is well. 'Night, Dolly

ഇന്ദ

Dear Dolly, Do you remember when my father used to hitch you to a sleigh in the snow and we would all go to find the perfect Christmas tree? Well, I had hoped that we could play in the snow with the horses here. The weather is not cooperating, though, because this Christmas was about 60 degrees and sunny. So much for my dreams, Dolly. Everyone here had extra carrots and Mrs. Pastures cookies. I thought of you and am mentally sending you a peanut butter and jelly sandwich, just like when I was a little girl. I know you don't get those in greener pastures. Merry Christmas, Dolly

ഇന്ദ

Chapter Eight
Shaikh, Joy And Sorrow

Dear Dolly, Ron heard about a gray Arabian mare that is for sale from one of his co-workers. We went to see that mare today. Her name is Buttons 'N Bows and they call her Shaikh. She is a beautiful horse, but for some reason she was very nervous around us. In her defense, the weather was cold and windy and we were new to her. I was told that Shaikh has been used primarily as a broodmare, but the man who owns her said that he has ridden her on trail rides all over Tennessee. But get this, Dolly: when he tried to mount her, he couldn't get her to stand still, so he tied her to a post and got on her. Once he was on, he leaned down and untied Shaikh as she walked off. How unsafe can that be? That's a major concern and it will require some training if we buy Shaikh.

We're going to take some time to think about this decision. I don't want to rush into anything. Wouldn't you know that when I need you, there you stand, grazing away at the eternal grass without a care in the world. Sometimes that sounds so tempting, but I don't have a taste for grass. 'Night, Dolly

ଛୠ

Dear Dolly, We did it! After two whole weeks of soul-searching, we brought Shaikh home to live at Summerwind. She was agitated after the trailer ride, so I put her in the arena after I wormed her to let her get acclimated to her new surroundings. Shaikh has excellent bloodlines and if we want to raise babies we need to concentrate on mares of this quality. We already have a great start with Maria and Lilli. But Shaikh also needs to be rideable, don't you think?

Today we rode Shaikh and she will need some work. She really does have a problem with standing still to be mounted. Lord knows you stood still, sometimes even when I wanted you to move. And Lilli and Maria are both planted like concrete when I mount. But Shaikh is a different story.

She started spinning the minute I put my foot in the stirrup. I remembered what I had read about pushing her flanks away from me, making her turn at my will, not hers. I did this several times, until just the slightest pressure had Shaikh moving. Then I re-positioned her to stand for mounting. It took at least twenty attempts before I was able to get on her.

Once I was on Shaikh she was great, listening to my cues and behaving herself. I think with some work this problem can be overcome. I had no trouble dismounting, but as you know, most horses are glad to stand still for you to get off their backs! Shaikh behaved admirably. I'd be willing to bet that Shaikh has been kicked in the sides or bumped on her back when someone tried to mount her. If you think about it, I can't imagine that having someone tie you to a post and mount that way is any fun. 'Night, Dolly

ಐ೦೮

Dear Dolly, Shelby arrived yesterday and took Maria and Shaikh back with her. I am going to have them bred to her stallion (the same one who is the sire of Diamahn 'Lil). I don't like having Maria away from me, but hopefully it won't be for very long. I would love for Maria to have a baby that looks like her and has her docile personality.

With Maria and Shaikh gone, I am now concentrating my time on riding Lilli. She doesn't show any signs of stiffness in her joints, but she is still kicking out with her hind leg at the most inopportune moments. Today she kicked out so hard that she knocked one of the boards in the arena completely out. Just when I think Lilli is going to be good, she jolts me back into reality. I've even tried to ride her bareback just in case the saddle is bothering her. But I'll keep working on her, because I still have hopes that she can be the horse she was when we lived in North Carolina. 'Night, Dolly

જી C8

Dear Dolly, Well, the good news is that both Shaikh and Maria are in foal. But the bad news is that Maria has conceived twins. I understand that this can be disastrous for a mare, and that most twin foals don't survive. The vet said to wait until the thirty-day ultrasound to see if both embryos are still there, and if so, he will flush one. This waiting is terrible, especially since Maria is so far away.

To get my mind off Maria, I worked with Diamahn 'Lil in the round pen today. I have an unusual problem with her. When I try to get her to run away from me, she comes and stands close beside me. Nothing I do will make her move away from me. Dolly, what do I do? I have tried all those techniques I read about to get Diamahn 'Lil to move away from me. Maybe I need someone not one so bonded to get her to move out. Is it possible that you can imprint *too* much?

Shelby called to say that the thirty-day ultrasound showed that Maria lost both embryos. I'm really disappointed, but I'm going to go visit her next week, if you can do without me. Shelby has her hands full and needs some help. I'll tell you about my visit when I get home. Don't try to fly with me, Dolly, because if you go to North Carolina I'm afraid you won't want to come back. 'Night, Dolly

જી C8

Dear Dolly, What a trip! When I drove up, Maria greeted me with her beautiful low whinny and Shaikh turned her back and walked away. There were horses everywhere; some were Shelby's and some were new ones I didn't recognize. Shelby explained that she had taken in one horse that was ill and another one for training. She had two new foals and three yearlings that had been pastured at a neighbor's house until the night before. When these horses were added to her usual inventory of Arabian horses and Pete the mule, it made for quite a circus. In addition, there were Maria and Shaikh to deal with. Maria should come back into season next week and we hope for a better outcome this time.

I did get to work with both horses in the arena. As usual, Maria was great until Pete started chasing all the pasture-kept horses. Over and around they went and try as I might to keep Maria focused, I couldn't get her attention off the steeplechase in the woods. So I stopped. There was just too much disruption.

The next day everything was back to normal and both horses did extremely well. Shaikh no longer walked away every time I tried to mount her and I considered that a major accomplishment. I wish I could have had a longer visit, but when I spoke with Ron on the fourth day, I could hear the fatigue in his voice. Horse-keeping is a lot of physical work even if you don't have a job away from home, as Ron does. And of course I missed you, Dolly. I decided to come home and wait for the results of Maria's breeding here. Besides, there is always plenty to keep me busy at Summerwind. 'Night, Dolly

ഇറ

Dear Dolly, I can't imagine a worse thing than to have the phone ring with the devastating news I received this afternoon. Shortly before 5:00 p.m. Shelby called to say that Shaikh had colicked and was not responding to the vet's treatments at all. I spoke with her vet, who said that the outlook looked grave. Shaikh had some sort of intestinal blockage and even tubing didn't help. There was a lot of resistance when he pushed the tube in and the oil came back out of her mouth. He suggested taking her to the University of Tennessee for surgery, but he warned that her chances weren't good and she would surely lose the foal. I struggled with this scenario, with common sense guiding me for the most part. I had not insured Shaikh as I had Lilli and Maria, partially because her purchase price was very low. However, I had planned to insure her later when we had rebounded from Lilli's hospital bill. I talked the situation over with Ron, who said that I had to make the ultimate decision. It was very difficult, being so far away from the horses. At 11:00 p.m., after Shaikh had been unresponsive for almost twelve hours, I told the vet to go ahead and put her down. He said that he would work with her for a while longer and if she showed the slightest sign of improvement, he would call me.

I didn't sleep that night, waiting for a call that didn't come. At 7:00 a.m., Shelby called to let me know that Shaikh had been put down around 4:00 a.m. and that they had buried her on their farm by the creek. I was deeply saddened by her death and even more heartbroken over the precious little life that would never come to be. I know you're sad too, Dolly. I'll let you go back to your clouds now. 'Night, Dolly

ଈୠଔ

We learned from the vet who attended Shaikh that he felt certain that Shaikh had experienced problems with worms in the past. I do know that the seller had been unclear about her de-worming history, but I had been so anxious to make Shaikh my own that I didn't seek more definite answers to my questions.

It is very important to have your horses on a regular de-worming program. The following tips work for me:

> ଔ Alternate worming products with each worming. If you use the same product each time, the worms will develop an immunity to the medicine.

> ଔ Try to worm at least every eight weeks and administer the wormer when the horse has no access to food of any kind.

> ଔ In September, make sure that you give the horse a boticide to kill the bot eggs that stick to the horse's coat and may be ingested at this time of the year.

Dear Dolly, I had begun to be anxious about Maria being so far away from me and was willing to forget the breeding just to have her home, safe and sound. But Shelby had good news

89

when I called today. Maria had been bred and would be bred again in two days. She said that we could either leave Maria until the sixteen-day ultrasound or we could come and get her. We decided to pick her up. We would worry about her pregnancy later.

Ron's father came and horse-sat for us so that we could drive to Shelby's last weekend to get Maria. Once there, we loaded Maria and drove straight back to Tennessee. The round trip took us sixteen hours and we were both exhausted, but we had our Maria home. Now all we had to do was wait for the results of the sixteen-day ultrasound.

The ultrasound revealed twins. The vet said he would advise flushing one and I jokingly told him to make sure to leave a filly. We were anxious until the thirty-day ultrasound, anticipating that Maria would resorb the fetus again. But on day thirty, the one beautiful embryo was still there. That was the start of our miracle baby!

The vet continued to monitor Maria's hormone levels, and now he says that she has as much chance to carry to full term as any other mare. At the age of eleven, Maria is a maiden mare, so naturally we will be cautious about every incident during her pregnancy, as she has no foaling history.

I am still very sad about Shaikh's death and the loss of the foal. But I am so happy that Maria is going to have that little filly (wishful thinking) to run and play alongside her mother. Think baby thoughts and I'll talk to you soon. 'Night, Dolly

ഇന്ദ

ය Maria's situation is really not that uncommon. About 50 per cent of ovulations result in a mare releasing more than one egg follicle. While twin conceptions do occur, they account for only five percent of pregnancies and usually result in abortion or the birth of stillborn foals. For this reason, an ultrasound should be performed at 16 days post-cover.

ය If twins reflect, most vets will advise flushing or pinching one of the ova. This procedure will enable the mare to carry the fetus to full term.

‍ cs Also, the tendency toward twinning is believed to be inherited and a mare that has a history of twinning will probably continue to do so in the future, as will her filly offspring.

Dear Dolly, With me being preoccupied with Shaikh's tragic death and Maria's breeding problems, Lilli had been home free. She had recuperated nicely from her illness and I was once again attempting to ride her. Lilli was her usual self in the round pen, but now she really stutter-kicked in the trot. I became disheartened with Lilli and felt that I needed some positive feedback from a horse. With this in mind, I concentrated on riding Maria.

Dolly, I know that this was not the right way to handle the situation, but Maria is so easy to ride and we have developed such a strong bond. In contrast, it seemed like every time I tried to work with Lilli, I came away depressed. This is not the reason I got into the horse business in the first place. I have to get my attitude toward Lilli in check before it gets out of hand. I could use some input because, after all, you are a horse. 'Night, Dolly

ഹോൽ

Chapter Nine
The Barn Grows

Dear Dolly, Did you hear the news? We are going to build an addition to the barn. We have been planning for this since we purchased the property. It became even more important when we separated the one stall we had for birthing when Diamahn 'Lil was weaned. And like most horse owners who fill the barn with as many horses as they have stalls, I want more horses.

Today Ron drew a picture of the new barn and we both liked the design. He will plan the structure and I will design the floor plan. We are going to shop for the materials to begin the construction this weekend. I am so excited, because in addition to a new birthing stall, we will have one more box stall and a big tack room. Another perk will be a large loft for hay storage. The old barn had a very small loft and we had to store our hay in the basement of our house. I know you've seen us hauling one bale at a time with the garden tractor. That's always good for a laugh.

Of course, the birthing stall is our first priority, but the tack room is second on our wish list. We spend a lot of time at the barn, especially during the foal watches, and we also really like to sleep in the barn, even when there is no reason to do so. The tack room will be directly across the hall from the birthing stall, and it will have a Plexiglas observation window so that we can watch the mare without disturbing her. That way, I can sit and watch the horses and listen to the sounds as they eat their meals. Best of all, I can hear the night sounds they make. Isn't farm life grand? 'Night, Dolly

ꕥ

Dear Dolly, I could not have asked for a better father-in-law. He helped with the construction of the first part of the barn and even after all that work and punishment, he is eager to pitch in and assist with the addition. The work is going well and today Ron put the roof on the loft. It's scary to see him standing on the high roof, working without a care in the world. I get a nosebleed just going up there, and I usually crawl on my hands and knees because I'm afraid to stand upright. We do have a weathervane for the top of the roof, but Ron said that he would have to gain a little more courage before he attempted to put it there.

One thing I *can* take credit for was the idea of putting a built-in bench in the hallway of the new addition. Ron built a great bench that opens for storage, and I plan to put the horses' grooming supplies and first aid kit in it. Glad I thought of it. 'Night, Dolly

೮೦೦೪

Dear Dolly, Can we take a minute to reflect? Remember when I thought how great it would be if I didn't have to return to work immediately after moving to Tennessee? Well, here I am three years later and my 'temporary' break from work is still going strong. Never in my wildest dreams did I expect to be content to stay at home and dress in a t-shirt and jeans every day. I wonder how long I can keep up this temporary arrangement.

We are almost finished with the construction of the barn itself, but the tack room will have to wait until later. My target date for the completion of Maria's birthing stall is March 1, and that is only two weeks away. I have read that it is important to give a pregnant mare time to get acclimated to the new stall. Since Maria has not had a foal before, I don't know exactly how to predict her due date. The average time for gestation is 332 days, and that would make it June 10. But Lilli carried Diamahn just 329 days, so I guess I'll be watching Maria very closely for the last month and will be prepared for any surprises.

If you've wondered about all the hammering, Ron and I have been diligently working on the tack room that we said would have to wait, and it is almost finished now. We shopped for the best prices on paneling and flooring and are feeling good about our progress. With any luck, we will be able to sleep in the new room this weekend. 'Night, Dolly

೮೦೦೪

Chapter Ten
Whizteria, My Silver Lining

Dear Dolly, Since May of 1996, I have been following the progress of a little foal that I first saw imprinted on Shelby's farm. She has grown into a beautiful rose gray filly and her name is Whizteria. Her sire is SHF Southern Whiz, a champion out of South Carolina, and her sister is SF Pearlie Mae, 1996 World Champion mare in halter. I know this means absolutely nothing to you, but the drummer for the Rolling Stones, Charlie Watts, and his wife, Shirley, of Halsdon Arabians, own Pearlie Mae. Whizteria is triple registered and has great potential, but I only see her as the beautiful rose gray filly that I have watched grow up. Every time I visit or call Shelby, I make a point to ask about Whizteria. She has always been in the back of my mind, but the reality remains that she is out of my price range. Still, I can dream . . .

Shelby called last week and mentioned that when I was ready, she wanted to send me a tape of Whizteria, even though she knew I wasn't planning on buying another horse right away. Shelby knew that I had my heart set on another gray mare, but the tragedy with Shaikh was still fresh in my mind. I told her to go ahead and send it to me anyway – I know for a fact that dreams are free.

Anyway, Dolly, I wanted to thank you for watching the tape with me today. Oh, I'm so in love with this horse. Whizteria is now a beautiful three-year-old. She is still rose gray with a black mane and tail. She should turn completely white as she gets older, but isn't she exotic, Dolly? Watch her run – isn't she fluid? She makes me wish I had known Maria as a three-year-old, because they have the same movement. Still, I know I am only dreaming, because I can't afford Whizteria. We'll look at the tape from time to time, though. It never hurts to dream. 'Night, Dolly

ഇൻയ

Dear Dolly, You will never believe your ears! Shelby called just to chat (she said). She has become my sounding board regarding the horses, especially Lilli. Shelby doesn't think that Lilli is making progress and has suggested that I might want to consider selling her. She also said that since Lilli has developed unexplained problems under saddle, I would probably want to sell her solely as a broodmare. Lilli has the exotic, dished face that is so desired by Arabian horse owners and she produces beautiful babies. I told Shelby that I would think about selling Lilli, but that I wasn't ready to give up on her yet. In passing, she remarked, "Maybe you should sell Lilli and buy Whizteria." "Boy," I thought, "wouldn't that be great! I seem to be going backwards with Lilli and all I need is a three-year-old to train." But Shelby pointed out that Whizteria would be a clean slate, eager to learn. I knew her history and where she grew up, so there should be no unpleasant surprises.

But I cautioned myself not to get my hopes up, because I knew what the appraisal had been on Whizteria when she was a tiny foal. She would surely be out of my reach now. Still, it didn't hurt to ask the price, so I did. Instead of giving me a figure, Shelby told me to think about what I could do, and she would do the same.

Two days later, Shelby left a message on my answering machine as to the amount of cash she would take. Although her offer was generous, it was still beyond my comfort level. Shelby also said that she would be willing to accept terms on Whizteria, so without thinking I said, "It's a shame you don't like jewelry!" Without skipping a beat, Shelby asked, "What kind of jewelry?" I explained that when I lived in the material world, I had bought many nice pieces of jewelry. Others I had received as gifts. The piece I had in mind was my wedding band.

Now, Dolly, I know that sounds cold and callous, but it was a ring that I had custom made when Ron and I decided to remarry. It was designed from various diamonds, but it had no particular meaning for me. Then, too, I no longer worked and obviously I didn't need fancy jewelry in the barn. If there was a choice to be made at this point in my life between expensive jewelry and a horse, the horse would win - hands down.

I told Shelby that I had a written appraisal on the ring, and the replacement value and the market value were both more than she was asking for Whizteria. Mind you, market value is strictly what a buyer is willing to pay and the seller is willing to accept. Dolly, imagine my utter disbelief when Shelby said that she would take the trade, the ring sight unseen. If I had ever doubted our friendship before, I didn't now. Who in their right mind would make a trade like that, if not a true friend? Shelby told me that she would transfer the papers and mail them to me. The only thing that she asked of me was that I obtain insurance on Whizteria.

Shelby called the next afternoon and told me that she had signed the papers and express mailed them to me. I was elated and immediately called my insurance agent and obtained full coverage on Whizteria. I could hardly believe that the beautiful rose gray filly I had admired and watched grow for three years was now mine!

I insured the ring and sent it along with the appraisal, and a San Marcos bracelet thrown in for "good measure" to Shelby. When I moved away from North Carolina, she had given me a gold pyramid pendant representing the Egyptian Arabian heritage. That particular day, I was wearing the San Marcos bracelet and Shelby had remarked that her mother had given her one when she was young, but the clasp kept breaking and she had lost it. She was surprised and pleased when she received it. Shelby loved the ring, but said that she felt so guilty about taking my wedding band. I told her that I could care less about the ring, because it got me what I had dreamed about. Besides, a diamond ring can't nuzzle me or call out to greet me the way Whizteria will.

I am going to Shelby's barn in April to work with Whizteria. Shelby gave sixty days' training with the transfer and a free breeding for Lilli, or another mare if I so choose. So, although I'm worried about leaving Maria in her final stages of pregnancy, I can't wait to get there and ride my horse. Ron is taking vacation time to horse-sit so that I can take the trip without guilt, if that's possible.

I am sure that you share my joy in making Whizteria a part of our family. It's just one more horse for you to watch over and I guarantee that you will love her. 'Night, Dolly

જીભ

Dear Dolly, I hope you have been taking care of things at Summerwind while I've been in North Carolina working with Whizteria. Let me fill you in.

When I arrived, Whizteria was in her stall, all clean and clipped and gorgeous. Whizteria had been pasture kept for the majority of her life, and Shelby warned me about the filly's stall habits – basically, she is a pig, but I think she will be worth the trouble, don't you?

Shelby had started Whizteria in hunt seat, and she had been riding her for the two months since I had become her owner. Now it was my turn. I had always ridden Western or bareback, so this close-contact style was completely new to me. I lunged her and she responded to my commands easily. Whizteria did have trouble distinguishing between my use of the words "whoa" and "walk," so Shelby suggested that I use "walk on" instead. This seemed to work well for Whizteria. I sacked her out with a feed sack, as Shelby had taught me to do with all my horses, and then it was time to ride.

I had to get a leg up from Shelby, and it's a good thing I got past the feeling that I needed to hold onto the Western saddle horn, or I would have been in big trouble. I'll get a mounting block when I get back home. Besides, since I had the surgery, I need a boost getting on most of the time, anyway.

Whizteria was like magic, and she seemed to float when she trotted. I could not believe she had just turned three. I was a little worried about posting, having ridden only Western, but Shelby said that she would work with me in the limited time we had and that I could go back home and practice on another horse. She didn't want Whizteria to be confused if I didn't "get it" on her right away.

I attempted to post and I could get it some of the time, then a couple of strides wouldn't be right. All of this proper riding was complicated; I just rode you, Dolly, without even thinking about leg position or stirrup length. But I'll get it sooner or later. I did decide to practice posting on Lilli instead of Whizteria until I master it. I don't want to mess this horse up with my inability to get the rhythm.

I'm also working on keeping my hands down. It's a struggle to remember, because every time Whizteria trots, I automatically raise my hands. Shelby suggested that I hold onto Whizteria's saddle pad until I can resolve my problem.

The exciting news is that Shelby is going to deliver Whizteria tomorrow and take Lilli back for breeding. Oh, no! When Shelby picks Lilli up, I will lose my posting horse. Maria is too pregnant and Diamahn 'Lil is still a yearling. What to do, what to do? Sometimes there's just too much worry around Summerwind. 'Night, Dolly

ဆာထ

Dear Dolly, Well, what do you think of our gray girl? Shelby and her mother just left with Lilli, so I thought I would take a minute to tell you about Whizteria's arrival.

Whizteria made herself right at home when I put her in her stall. Shelby suggested that I might want to put her in the side paddock to let her stretch her legs. The other horses were so excited about a strange horse in the barn that Diamahn 'Lil ran right into the side of the run-in shed. Aside from a few cuts and bruises, Diamahn 'Lil was all right, but the worst injury was to the shed itself. She knocked two boards completely out.

After all the horses were brought in for the night, Ron ordered pizza and Shelby and her mother visited with us for a little while before they turned in. I woke them at 5:00 a.m., because they had a long trip ahead of them and Shelby was anxious to get back home. She has the same difficulty that Ron and I have finding someone to feed her horses when she's away. After we had coffee and doughnuts, Shelby went to the barn to get Lilli ready for the trip and to say good-bye to Whizteria. As I entered the barn, I heard Shelby saying to Whizteria, "Now, you be a good girl for Emily. You'll have a good home with lots of love." Truer words could not be spoken. Whizteria is my silver lining.

Dolly, I can use all the watching over that I can get as I take on the responsibility of training a three-year-old. Ron always insists that we are not horse trainers and I get really upset when he says that. Anyone who owns a horse is a trainer and you never stop learning. But that's another story and I'm ready for sleep. 'Night, Dolly

ജ⚬യ

Chapter Eleven
Maria's Summer Miracle

Dear Dolly, Good news! Shelby called today and said that Lilli had come into season and that they were breeding her today. They will breed her three times and wait for the magical sixteen-day ultrasound. If Lilli is in foal, she can come home then. Meanwhile, I am beginning to ride Whizteria a little each day. We are getting used to each other and so far, she is doing great! She has taken over the number-one position in the pecking order, since Maria is confined to the paddock for the remainder of her pregnancy. The real test of the pecking order will be when Lilli arrives back on home soil. 'Night, Dolly

&os

Dear Dolly, Ron left early yesterday morning bring Lilli home. He spent the night with Shelby and her husband before heading back to Tennessee. I was really glad to see the trailer coming up the driveway, not only because I missed Lilli, but because I can now practice my posting.

Strangely, though, Lilli seemed very nervous when she backed out of the trailer. Ron left her in the aisleway of the barn while I added shavings to her stall, but I think she must have made a comment to Maria about her being fat. Whatever the case, Maria struck out at Lilli, putting her foot through the metal gate and cutting her leg in the process. We were able to doctor Maria on our own, being the injury experts we now are. I have to be careful, though, not to become too confident with my limited medical knowledge. It's important that I know the difference between the kind of injury that we can treat and the kind that needs a vet's attention. Help me to keep a close eye on Lilli. 'Night, Dolly

&os

Dear Dolly, This is yet another time of frustration. Why can't things be the way they were when we rode across the fields, Dolly? I put Lilli in the round pen today, and she immediately started to run completely out of control. Lilli has always been perfect with the ground exercises and even if I couldn't always count on her for a perfect ride, I could look forward to the round pen exercises. I tried to calm her, because I was worried about her possibly losing the foal. She was totally soaked with sweat, so I put a lead on her and walked her around the round pen for ten minutes.

When Lilli was cooled out, I mounted her to work on the much-anticipated posting. What once had been a little stutter step now became a full-fledged kick. When I put Lilli into a trot, she would trot a few steps and then kick with that same hind leg. To add insult to injury, she now put her head to the ground and rode the bit. The few times she trotted normally I was able to post, but just as I got into the rhythm, Lilli would kick again. It was almost as if she did it on purpose. Can a horse be that smart, Dolly? It didn't get any better, so I ended the session in despair and have decided to seek professional help with posting. 'Night, Dolly

ಬಂಡ

Dear Dolly, I was introduced to a young man, Phillip, who trains Arabian horses in the area and I asked him if he taught old people to post. He just laughed and said that one of his best students was seventy years old and was riding for the first time. Feeling encouraged, I made an appointment with him for the next day.

Phillip was an excellent instructor. Once again I got in the rhythm for four or five strides, but then I would completely lose it. He commented that it was easy for children to get the rhythm because they had nothing with which to compare it. He said that usually adults would over-think and try too hard. That was exactly what I was doing. Phillip further said that one day a light would come on in my head, and I would just "get it." I wanted that day to arrive and made another appointment on the spot.

The day before my next lesson, I was bringing the horses in for their feeding. It was a very blustery, cold day and it had rained all week. Ron had gone to the animal shelter and found a beautiful part Border Collie, part Dalmatian puppy that we named Molly and her assignment was to be my barn buddy. When I went out to open the gate for the horses, Molly followed me, barking noisily. I suppose Molly thought she should go round them up for me.

The horses came inside the gate, but they were excited and Diamahn 'Lil started to run back out. Molly started chasing her and Diamahn 'Lil was running fast, so there was no time for me to get out of the way. Diamahn 'Lil ran over me on the way out, pushing me into the gate. She stepped right on the top of my foot. I usually laugh my injuries off, but I knew immediately that this one was serious. The pain was almost unbearable, but somehow I was able to hobble around and get the feeding completed. In the meantime, Molly was a happy puppy, probably because she considered herself successful in running the horses out of the paddock! I went back to the house and waited for the pain to subside.

Dolly, I was so looking forward to tomorrow and my next posting lesson, but now I'm going to have to cancel. Maybe I'll be better next week. Wish my pain away for me. 'Night, Dolly

ಬೃಂದ

Dear Dolly, I guess you noticed that the foot didn't get any better by itself. I hobbled around for three weeks and watched my foot turn every color in the rainbow, until I could no longer cope with the pain. I have a stubborn streak where the doctor is concerned! I finally called a podiatrist, who x-rayed my foot and said that I had broken it. It wasn't a critical break as far as mobility goes, but it had to be placed in a soft cast for three weeks. Maybe one day I'll learn to go to the doctor right away instead of wasting valuable time, not to mention suffering needless pain. Now, to my dismay, the posting lessons will have to wait for a while longer. Feel a little pity for me, won't you? 'Night, Dolly

ಬೃಂದ

Dear Dolly, I'm finally able to wear a shoe without excruciating pain, so it's back to riding again. My concentration has been on Whizteria. I'm really excited about working with her, because I know something will be learned by both of us. I lunged her and put her through her paces exactly as I had done when I was at Shelby's and everything went smoothly. Most of the time there were no incidents, but I soon learned that when Whizteria was in season she became spookier. So I continued to sack her out with each session. I introduced Whizteria to trash cans, plastic bags, cavaletti poles and anything else I could find to make the lesson interesting.

The most incredible thing happened today, Dolly. When I finished riding Whizteria, I took her back to the barn and left her in the hallway while I went to open the side gate. She was still completely tacked up; when I came back, there was no Whizteria! I was totally baffled, because the hallway was secure (or so I thought.) Leave it to a three-year-old to get my adrenaline pumping. Whizteria had decided to investigate the feed room in the short time that I was gone.

Now the feed room is only about eight feet wide, with hay on one side and metal cans full of sweet feed on the other. Whizteria had about three feet of space with which to navigate. She had simply stepped right up into the feed room and was having some hay to eat. I didn't want her to panic, as I was completely aware of the potential for a wreck here. So I just started backing Whizteria up the same way she would back out of a trailer. It worked! Ron happened to come home at the same time and could not believe his eyes. We joked about Whizteria taking the initiative to practice Horse Trailer Loading 101. I really could use your help in baby-sitting this horse. She's far too curious. 'Night, Dolly

෨෬

Dear Dolly, It's getting close to Maria's due date, so today I started to prepare her stall for foaling. Since this is to be her first foal, there can be a wide variation between the due date and the actual birth date. But life goes on and I couldn't stop working with the other horses just because Maria's having a baby.

So I worked with Whizteria while keeping one eye on the paddock where Maria is confined for the duration of her pregnancy. Since the weather is so hot and humid now, I am giving Maria the run of the hallway (with the feed room door closed, of course) for shelter from the hot sun. She loves to stand in the cool hallway most of the time now. I'm catering to Maria as much as I can, because I remember how uncomfortable I was when my babies were due – and they didn't weigh one hundred pounds.

After I rode Whizteria, I attempted to ride Lilli. I say *attempted,* because Lilli is really acting weird in the early stages of pregnancy. She stutter-kicked when trotting and seems really nervous and excitable. She has also taken on a stallion-like attitude, even trying to mount the other horses. I was so concerned that I called the vet. He explained that a lot of mares do this because of hormone imbalance. He said that this behavior should get more normal as time went by, but that one of his mares acted this way up until the day of delivery. I thanked him for the encouraging words and the hope. He has a dry sense of humor, but then I do, too.
'Night, Dolly

෨෬

Dear Dolly, Just when I'm feeling smug about my training abilities, something always brings me back to reality. Today Whizteria was far from perfect on the lunge. She started running as fast as she could when I put her into a trot. I stopped her and started over and she did the same thing. She acted as though she had seen a ghost. After stopping and starting her a few times, she grew bored and behaved herself. I'm sure this behavior will keep me on my guard. I talked to Shelby, who said that Whizteria was simply testing me and that I had passed the test. Whizteria is an extremely intelligent youngster, so I will have to keep on my toes to be a step ahead. Riding her is like a dream; but not always . . .

Since the weather has been so hot, I have been working with Whizteria at dusk. This afternoon, I mounted her as usual after lunging. Shelby had suggested that I spend a lot of time on the walk, because she had seen so many horses that had been started at the trot without having been properly trained at the walk. She thought Lilli was one of those horses who may have been trained for endurance and had not been taught a slow walk. So for this reason, plus the fact that I was trying my best to start Whizteria correctly, I always started her at a walk.

After about fifteen minutes of walking, I applied pressure with my legs and asked for a trot, the same way I always did. This time, however, Whizteria pinned her ears (something I had never, ever seen her do) and continued to walk on. I tried several times, without success, to get her to trot. Finally, Ron suggested that he attach the lunge line and see if Whizteria would trot while on it. Whizteria obeyed, but she still pinned her ears and one time even attempted a little buck. I knew that something was not right with her and I suspected tooth trouble. I consulted one of my by now worn books and all of Whizteria's symptoms supported that theory.

I called the vet, who examined Whizteria and found that she had two loose molars that were wiggling around and were probably painful when the bit hit them. I felt terrible. Here I had been pushing her to trot and she was in pain. What a terrible owner I was. I was afraid she would never forgive me. It brought back a memory of a time when the equine dentist at Shelby's pulled two wolf teeth in Maria's mouth. I didn't expect to go riding right afterward, but Shelby said, "She's a horse, she'll get over it." I had felt guilty then, too.

I doctored Whizteria and in two days I tried to ride her again. I was delighted and relieved when we had a near-perfect workout. When I asked for a trot, she immediately responded to my cues. Whizteria is such a good horse; she continues to amaze me, even at her young age.

These are signs of tooth or mouth problems in horses:

- ❧ The horse may not perform well for you and may resist pressure to his mouth.

- ❧ He may demonstrate an unwillingness to respond to rein cues or he may respond by throwing his head up and down.

- ❧ The horse may drop food while chewing, so check for food on the floor of the stall. He may also turn his head to one side while chewing. In the worst case, if chewing causes the horse pain, he may not eat at all.

- ❧ Although horses of all ages can show loss of weight and poor coat condition, it is more prevalent in older horses.

- ❧ It is a good idea to have the horse's teeth floated at least once a year. I ask the vet to check our horses' teeth when he gives their semi-annual vaccinations in October.

Dear Dolly, Maria's due date has come and gone without incident. She is noticeably uncomfortable now. I groom her for a long time every morning and I take her carrots at midday. After all, she didn't choose to be in this predicament, did she? Why shouldn't she receive preferential treatment?

We started sleeping in the barn last night. You're more than welcome to join us, Dolly, but I have to warn you. All the horses and Ron snore, so you might want to rethink it. Besides, it's still too early to keep a twenty-four-hour vigil. We just want an excuse to sleep in the new tack room. The observation window is great, because I can get up during the night to check on Maria without her knowing it. We have even set up an intercom system that lets us hear even small sounds in the barn.

Everything seems very normal, except that Maria is getting bagged up and wax is forming on her nipples. How different from Lilli, who didn't show any signs of bagging or waxing. Maybe tonight will be special. 'Night, Dolly

ଞୠ

Dear Dolly, Each "tonight " turns into the next night. For two weeks, Maria has had wax on her nipples and today she has beads of milk. So I'll say it again: "Maybe tonight will be the night." Just for precaution, we will wrap her tail. It drags the ground, so wrapping the tail will be quite a feat. We are worrying Maria to death with our constant checks on her. But she is such a good girl and takes it all in stride. For the record, Maria never pins her ears at me. 'Night, Dolly

ଞୠ

Dear Dolly, Things are beginning to happen. Maria started to stream milk two days ago. I checked the contents of the foaling kit yet again as Ron wrapped Maria's tail with vetrap. He said that the muscles had relaxed on either side of her dock. We just knew that we had a baby on the way. But the night was a peaceful one, aside from Maria groaning and putting the fear of God in us every time she lay down.

Yesterday, Maria wouldn't eat hay and she made no attempt to go outside the barn in the morning, opting to stand in the hallway instead. I tried to groom her as per our usual routine, but she moved away from me as though she was uncomfortable with my being there. At midday, I took Maria carrots, but she turned them down. It was her lack of interest in carrots that confirmed the onset of labor. Maria's milk was streaming steadily now, so much so that her legs were wet. Her muscles were even more relaxed than before. The day went by slowly and I watched Maria like a mother hen. Ron wrapped her tail and we washed her backside in preparation. As a precautionary measure, we left the barn dogs in the basement and started the nightly vigil in the tack room.

As soon as the lights went out around 10:30 p.m., Maria started to pace. She would grab a bit of hay and walk all around the stall. Ron had drifted off to sleep immediately, so I sat by the window and watched Maria. For the first time, she noticed me in the window, because she would pace and stop at the stall door, looking at the window. It was as though she was asking me for help.

At 11:00 she laid down, only to get right back up. She did this twice more, each time a little faster. I decided to check on her and felt sweat on her shoulders. I went back into the tack room and woke Ron. I said, "If you want to see a baby born, wake up now!" We decided that the noise from the tack room door opening might surprise her if she was lying down. We were glad that we had built the bench in the hallway. This is where we would keep our vigil for the actual birth.

We had just sat down when we heard the unmistakable sound of Maria's water breaking. Immediately she went down again, this time to stay. Dolly, we had really put a lot of thought into the size of the foaling stall. At 24 x 14 feet, the mare has plenty of room to give birth without having to put the baby into a wall. Well, guess where that baby came out? Maria deposited the foal right against the wall underneath the waterer.

Ron and I were both so excited we could hardly sit still. We had uttered prayers while the birth took place, as we wanted a healthy foal and we wanted Maria to be okay. Although we were tempted to go in and immediately get involved, we knew from our experience with Diamahn 'Lil's birth that jabbering would do nothing for the solitude a birthing mare and foal deserved.

After a few moments' wait, we crept into the stall. At this point, we couldn't see anything but a very still form. I panicked, fearing that Maria's baby was dead. Tentatively, Ron got behind Maria and reached for the form, only to get poked by a tiny foot. It was moving and breaking the sac! Ron helped with that while I cried and complimented Maria on her beautiful baby. She was extremely proud and suddenly very slim! I retrieved towels and we dried the baby, but we couldn't tell what color it was, or even if it was a he or a she. I had jokingly told the vet to make sure he pinched the colt, but at this point I didn't care what the sex was. I just wanted a healthy baby.

Finally, after stumbling around in the dimly-lit stall, we realized that we would need more light if we were going to see anything. So I turned on the hallway light, and imagine our delight when we saw that we had a beautiful filly! The vet had done us proud! Now, you talk about a miracle, Dolly. We had one tonight out of an eleven-year-old maiden mare who had conceived and resorbed twins, conceived twins a second time, had one pinched, and presented us with this beautiful little filly. We were elated!

Dolly, you could have heard a pin drop in the barn while all of this was taking place! Not a horse made a noise, but rather they looked out their stall doors toward Maria's stall, in what I determined was a very respectful way. Animals sense what is going on, don't you think? Back to the story.

Within thirty-five minutes the little filly had stood, found her mother, nursed and taken a nap. We imprinted and it went very well. For a first-time mother, Maria handled all this without concern. We have a picture of Ron imprinting, with Maria standing by closely watching him. We used no restraint whatsoever with her. I was amazed!

I did worry through the night, not about the filly, but about Maria. She did not expel the afterbirth, something she should have done on her own. When we could see the sun creeping over the trees, I called the vet and left a message. He called back very shortly and said that he was heading our way and would check Maria and the new baby out.

When he arrived, he gave Maria a shot and within ten minutes she had dropped the afterbirth. He said that a lot of first-time mothers are very nervous and do not relax their muscles in a normal manner after giving birth. He conducted a thorough examination of the afterbirth and said that everything looked fine. The little filly stood very still while he examined her and was a perfect little lady. I might add that this vet's attitude toward newborn foals is a far cry from the one who examined Diamahn 'Lil for the first time. He was very gentle with the filly and talked to her the whole time he was looking her over. It made all the difference to the filly – and to me. The vet pronounced the filly "fit as a fiddle".

Most horse owners are fanatical about naming their horses, and I am no exception. I have been trying to think of the perfect name for Maria's new baby. I thought of the events over the past year: the incidents with the twins, Shaikh's death and Maria coming home to us safely. The filly was born on the first day of summer, so I decided to name the filly "Maria's Summer Miracle". We call her Summer for short. I hope that name meets with your approval, Dolly. I did think about naming her after you, but another horse cannot do you justice.

One last thing I want to tell you and I'll let you get some much-needed rest. (I wouldn't mind getting some, too.) Maria is a registered bay Arabian, but she is what is termed a "summer black". That means in the winter she is jet black, but she fades in the hot summer sun. For this reason, she can't be registered as a black. The filly is exactly the same color; her only markings are two white socks and a very tiny star. Shelby was shocked to learn that Summer didn't have a big star, blaze and snip, because the stallion has marked every other foal he has sired. I told you Summer is special. But she's not as special as you, Dolly. No horse will ever be. Sleep tight and say a prayer of thanks for our new baby.
'Night, Dolly

೩೦೦೮

Dear Dolly, You know, we were completely naïve during the birth of Diamahn "Lil, but this time around we know a little bit more about newborn foals. We imprinted several times with Summer. It just seems that everything fell into place with this filly; we are probably a little more relaxed now, don't you think? Mother and daughter are both doing fine, so today I went back to my training of Whizteria and Diamahn 'Lil. Whizteria is so funny, watching Summer over the fence for hours. Maybe it is because she is still a baby herself or that she wants a baby of her own, but she just stands there with

110

the most wistful look in her eyes. Maria will not let her touch noses with Summer yet, so Whizteria has to be content with just being close to her.

઼ఙ

Dear Dolly, Today we had a near-wreck with Summer. Maria had kept her close in the paddock for four weeks. When I had tried to turn them out into the bigger pasture earlier, Maria had made no effort to take Summer out into the world. But today was a beautiful, rain-free day and I decided that today was the day. The other horses were grazing contentedly in the upper pasture, so Maria and Summer quietly crept out of the paddock. "This is going well," I thought to myself. All of a sudden Whizteria noticed that the new baby was out and about, so she started running toward Maria and Summer. Naturally, the other horses followed suit. Maria took the baby and started running the other way, calling out to the other horses as she ran. I suppose she was telling them to keep their distance. But Whizteria was not having it. This was her first chance to actually touch the baby and she fully intended to do it!

They all ran up and down, up and down, and I'll admit I was afraid of what could have happened. The poor baby was terrified and exhausted. When the horses stopped running for a short time, the little filly stood panting. I seized that moment to call Maria, who knew just what to do. She came straight back to me and to the comfort of the paddock before any of the other horses caught up to her. I closed the gate with a bang and thanked God that no one was injured. I think a better way to introduce Summer to the herd is to let one or two horses come into the paddock each day to spend time with her. Then, when they are familiar with each other, I can turn them loose together in the big pasture. Does that sound like a plan? Boy, Dolly, life gets complicated doesn't it?
'Night, Dolly

઼ఙ

Dear Dolly, I wouldn't wish today on my worst enemies. You know that Summer has been grazing with the other horses in the big pasture for a while now. Up until today, she had grazed beside Maria and the other horses. So I felt especially content

111

with her progress as I drove away this morning to go to the post office.

I returned about one-and-a-half hours later and did not immediately go to check on Summer. I could see all the horses from the kitchen door and they were quietly grazing. It was about an hour before I grabbed carrots for the grown-ups and headed up the hill.

As I approached, I noticed blood on Summer's leg. I began to move faster toward her and was sickened by what I saw - most of the skin on her forehead hung loosely down between her eyes and blood was oozing. Trying to remain calm, I headed back to the barn as fast as I could. Maria, being the obedient horse that she is, followed along behind me with Summer by her side.

I immediately called the vet, who, as luck would have it, was just finishing with a farm call a few miles away. He said that he would be right out and to try to keep the little filly quiet until he arrived. Easier said than done! Somehow, I managed to get her to nibble some hay, but her mother stepped in and offered milk. That was the best calmative! I think Maria knew her baby needed help.

When the vet arrived, he examined and sedated Summer. Maria stood quietly in her stall where she could look into the hall where we had taken Summer. The vet said that the damage was severe, but that he would do the best that he could. He painstakingly cleansed and stitched the jagged cut. I was afraid to ask him if it would leave a scar. Here we had waited for this beautiful, miracle foal and now she was probably going to be scarred for life. I finally had the nerve to ask him and he said that we would hope for the best. Somehow that did not comfort me, but I knew that he had done all he could.

After the vet gave his parting instructions for Summer's care, I put her back into the stall with Maria. She immediately went to nurse and get a nuzzle from her mother. I was determined to find what had caused this terrible accident.

We had taken great precautions with the fencing and over the years had installed mesh fencing down both sides of our pasture. In fact, some of the cross-fencing was mesh fencing, so I knew that didn't cause this accident. Still I walked every foot of the fence to look for a break; there was none. Perplexed, I started to examine the cross-fencing in the upper pasture. That was when I saw the top high-tensile wire lying on the ground. I couldn't believe it! Somehow, Summer either got caught in the wire and snapped it from its cable, or been struck in the head when another horse had snapped it. Either way, she must have felt a tremendous blow.

The vet asked me if the electricity was on the wire that day. It had been turned off while I went to do my errands, and he suggested that a hot wire would probably have been a deterrent to her. I disagree, because if Summer had been caught in the wire, she would have been jolted over and over again. I don't want to think about what might have happened to her if that were the case. We're going to use mesh fencing instead of high-tensile wire from now on. I think that will be a much safer bet.

Hopefully, Summer will outgrow the scars. I have my doubts, but Shelby said that she had seen some terrible scars on foals that just went away as the foal grew. I hope that Summer lives up to her name and pulls this miracle off. As the vet said, we'll hope for the best. 'Night, Dolly

ଈଔଔ

Dear Dolly, I had a little surprise today. I haven't had the courage to look at Summer's scar for a few weeks, but today I felt brave. Even at her young age, she is blessed with a beautiful long forelock. I lifted that forelock and, lo and behold, the scar is disappearing nicely. I think that by the time she is grown, it will be unnoticeable. That really made my day, so I can go to bed with a smile. 'Night, Dolly

ଈଔଔ

Chapter Twelve
Trials And Tribulations

Dear Dolly, Things just go from bad to worse around here. We were finally recovering from the shock of Summer's injury when Diamahn' Lil got injured. I took her out of her stall one morning and I noticed that her back legs were swollen below the hock. She could hardly walk. Upon further examination, I saw that there were cuts and scratches all over her legs. I can't describe the guilt I felt for not noticing Diamahn 'Lil's injuries the night before when I brought her in. I usually do a check on all the horses, but last night I was in a hurry and didn't do what I should. I know she was in a lot of pain. I called the vet and while I waited for him to arrive, I went out to the pasture to look for the fence that surely did this to Diamahn 'Lil. Sure enough, a twenty-foot stretch of fence in the high pasture was completely down, thanks to the neighbor's cow, which was still grazing in our pasture. Diamahn 'Lil, always the horse to check any curious situation, had most likely gone over to see how he did it and had become entangled in the wire. Somehow, she had worked herself free, but not without serious consequences.

The vet once again made a visit to wrap legs and stitch wounds. He left me with various kinds of medication and I donned a nurse's cap once more. Diamahn 'Lil was confined to stall rest for three days and was not happy at all. I began to think about a way to make her happier and basically kill two birds with one stone.

Summer was now over four months old and I had to think about weaning her from Maria. She had started eating sweet feed at two weeks of age and was consuming a good portion of hay. I had also started taking Summer into a separate stall for the evening feeding and leaving her as long as she would allow before taking her back to Maria. I saw no indications that Summer wasn't ready to be weaned and I was sure that Maria was ready. The question had been who to enlist for baby-sitting.

After careful consideration of each horse's disposition, I decided that Diamahn "Lil was the one. She was closest in age and was laid back in mannerism, and was confined to stall rest while she recuperated from her leg injuries. I put Summer in the stall next door for the morning feeding and left her there while I took Maria out to pasture. Summer called out a few times, but having Diamahn 'Lil next door made all the difference in the world to her. Diamahn 'Lil seemed to be glad to have the companionship of another horse, even if it was a pesky four-month-old crybaby. Throughout the day, Summer had periods of panic when she needed to nurse and cried herself hoarse, but I kept the hay flowing and she soon calmed down. When she had those attacks, Maria would run the fence line for a while calling back, but soon she fell back into the pattern of grazing with the other horses. I was very pleased with myself for having this ingenious idea. That is, until two days later.

It was time for Diamahn 'Lil to go to the paddock, so I put Summer with her. By this time Summer had stopped calling for Maria and she was doing a little grazing beside Diamahn 'Lil. Unfortunately, Diamahn 'Lil had come into season and was more than a little irritable this particular morning. As the other horses came to the fence to meet Diamahn 'Lil and Summer and discuss what had been happening with them, Diamahn 'Lil kicked out at no one in particular. Wouldn't you know that Summer was standing directly in her line of fire?

Warily, I went out to check on her, thinking that it couldn't be as bad as the head cut. But at the top of her leg was a huge puncture wound that was dripping blood. Given our history of needing a vet, I had placed the vet on speed dial and was on a first-name basis with everyone in his office. Caller ID identified me and the receptionist answered by saying, "What happened?" As luck would have it, the vet was on a farm call near here, and he arrived within fifteen minutes. I jokingly told him that I felt we had not contributed enough to his children's education lately. He just laughed and said to wait until we got the bill for *this* injury.

As the vet was examining the wound, I commented that I didn't know that a kick could result in a puncture. He agreed it was not a common thing, but if a horse's hoof was jagged, it could happen. The treatment the vet prescribed requires antibiotics, stitches and nightly draining of the wound and treating with Nitrofurazone. But, miracle that Summer is, she is indeed living up to her name and is healing beautifully. We figure that by the time she is grown, she will be held together entirely by stitches! Say another prayer for Summer. 'Night, Dolly

ಬೂಡ

Dear Dolly, With this latest series of injuries, we prayed for normalcy at Summerwind. And for a short time, we got it. Then one night, we made our customary rounds before bedtime. Halfway to the barn, I heard loud thumps. My heart raced as I entered the barn, as I could not even speculate as to what this noise was being caused by. All the horses looked out their stall doors at me, with the exception of Diamahn 'Lil. She wasn't in a position to look, because she was down in the stall and couldn't get her feet under her (this is called being cast). Diamahn 'Lil has a habit of rolling before she rises, and this time she had rolled too far toward the wall. She didn't have enough room to get back over and her feet were against the stall wall. I always look back with malice to the vet who told me I read too much, but once again, I knew what to do.

116

If I had been alone I doubt that I would have been successful, but luckily Ron was home. I asked him to get a rope and tie it around the hind leg closest to the wall. I took hold of the front leg on the same side, then asked him to start rocking Diamahn 'Lil, which he did, until she was able to move around and get up on her own. But, as Ron can tell you, you need to get out of the way quickly when the horse gets up.

I am sorry to say that Diamahn 'Lil didn't learn her lesson that night, because she did the same thing the next night. What is amazing is that she never once panicked, and I think that she would have waited patiently until we came to rescue her. Diamahn 'Lil trusted that we would help her and that says a lot for a two-year-old.

Let's hope that Diamahn 'Lil will grow out of this present situation soon. I don't need gray hairs. 'Night, Dolly

ഇരു

Dear Dolly, I kept thinking that everything that could happen had – until Sunday afternoon when Ron sprayed insecticide for wasps in the run-in-shed. The horses were far away in the high pasture when he sprayed, but within a half hour we noticed that they had made their way down for water. Ron ran to the gate to shut them out of the shed, but it was too late. Diamahn 'Lil stood at the fence, foaming at the mouth with her neck extended. I felt inside her mouth and nothing seemed to be lodged. I called the vet, who by now knew me by the sound of my voice. He asked if we had anything poisonous in the pasture. It suddenly occurred to me that Diamahn 'Lil had gone into the shed and had probably swallowed insecticide. The vet told us to give Diamahn 'Lil lots of water and to keep a close watch on her.

I've learned another lesson and will make certain that all future spraying is done far away from any area that horses can access. That was a close call! 'Night, Dolly

ഇരു

Dear Dolly, When I was a little girl, I remember watching dad work on your feet, but I don't remember whether or not he also used a farrier's services. Since he had his own anvil, he must have shod you himself. This leads me to tell you about the trouble we have had finding good farriers since we moved here. When I was in North Carolina, Shelby used her farrier and sent me a bill. But since we moved here, we have had terrible luck with farriers.

The first one kicked Lilli in the stomach when she lost her balance. I am very aware that farriery is dangerous and wouldn't do it for any amount of money. But you don't kick a horse, let alone a pregnant horse. It has taken two years for Lilli to let another farrier trim her feet. The second farrier came out several times, but then he was kicked in the head by his neighbor's filly and is no longer in the business. The third farrier came highly recommended, made two appointments and failed to show. The fourth farrier was also a trainer. We had a good relationship for a year and the horses were really beginning to feel comfortable with him. But then he decided to devote his time to training and I was back to searching for a farrier again.

Then one day, I took my wonder dog, Molly, to the vet for her shots. I spotted a business card on the bulletin board with a "new in business" note. I asked the receptionist if she knew the farrier; it turns out he was her daughter's fiancé and was trying to build up his business. She said that he would call me. Considering our track record with farriers, I thought, "Sure he will." But that night, the farrier did call and he is truly a godsend. He is newly married and his wife came out with him for the first time today. I think we will become good friends. So you see, miracles do happen at Summerwind. 'Night, Dolly

೫ಅೞ

Dear Dolly, It's funny how I took every aspect of farm life for granted when I was a child. Dad baled the hay and you ate it. Well, here it's different; you have to go looking for hay. Not only that, but you have to look high and low for good quality hay, and there is plenty of it that lacks in quality. Ron found a source through someone he works with when we moved to Summerwind. The first year the hay was excellent; the second year it lacked in quality and was moldy, which we knew could make any horse sick and cause pregnant mares to abort.

So we were extremely careful as to what we gave the horses out of the bales and we wasted a lot of hay and money. On the third year, we began to look for another source. Now we finally have enough contacts to get good hay, which is one less thing to worry about. When you have broodmares, hay quality can get very critical and we do not want to take any chances. Speaking of hay, have some grass on me. 'Night, Dolly

છ૦ભ

We had to rely on others to help us choose hay when we started horsekeeping. We learned the hard way that all hay is not created equal. This guide will help you choose the right type of hay:

- Look for hay that is green, leafy and sweet smelling. Don't just smell the outside of the bale, but ask the seller to break the bale open so that you can check the inside.

- Don't accept hay that has any hint of mold. This hay usually has some gray or black areas and should be avoided. It will be difficult to split the bale into individual flakes and they may be matted together.

- Avoid hay that has weeds and plants that can't be identified. It may be toxic to the horses and have little nutritional value.

- A good bale of hay should bounce slightly when it is dropped. If it lands like a rock, question its quality.

Dear Dolly, This is not my favorite topic, but if you have horses, you have to talk about manure management. At first we had trouble making a decision about how to dispose of the mountain of manure that we accumulated in just a short time. We had conducted a lot of research on how to best handle it and finally decided that we could utilize the manure best by composting. We could then use the compost for gardening and fertilizing. Ron built three large bins that we emptied the manure into. The first one accommodates fresh manure and shavings. While the decomposition time is longer with shavings, we found that they are the best bedding option for our stalls.

The contents of the first bin are turned into the second bin after two weeks; and the third after a month. This is a continuous cycle, and the third bin is the one used for the garden and to fertilize the lawn and pastures. Initially, we thought that we could never use all that manure, but we have always found somebody or someplace that needs it. We received several excellent pamphlets from our agricultural service when we were weighing our options. That's all the poop for now. 'Night, Dolly

ଧଓଓ

Dear Dolly, I am very frustrated with Ron and his blind spot when it comes to trailer loading. From the time that Diamahn 'Lil was very small, I mentioned to him that we needed to load her lots of times so that she would always load with no problem. Every time I asked, he would have something else to do. It has been the same situation with Summer. And now Lilli is due to have another foal and none of them will be trailer loaded. Ron believes that when the horses become adults, they will load without any trouble. Dolly, he is so wrong about this. I should have learned how to hitch the trailer to the truck, but I don't think I can load the babies without Ron's help. I just know we are headed for a wreck. Keep your hooves crossed. 'Night, Dolly

ଧଓଓ

Dear Dolly, Doesn't Lilli look just like a Puffalump? She evidently got into a hornet's nest or something, because she came in from the pasture looking very swollen, with lots of sting marks all over her body. Our new family member, the vet, was already here checking one of the other horses, so he put salve on Lilli's bites. The next day, her legs were covered with sores, so the vet suggested we put calamine lotion on the bites and eventually Lilli should show no signs of the stings. I hope so. 'Night, Dolly

ଧଓଓ

Dear Dolly, We made it through the winter without injury. The most difficult thing I have had to get used to is the ice that forms in the outside water tanks. Every morning, I clunk away with a pick-ax until the horses have water to drink. I did manage to keep one tank de-iced electrically, but I'm really nervous about that method, because I've heard that touching a de-icer in a metal tank can shock a horse. So far, that hasn't happened. Luckily, the sun usually thaws the other tanks by mid-afternoon. Then the whole process starts over the next morning. But I can see spring coming, so we'll be okay. 'Night, Dolly

৩০০৪

Chapter Thirteen
A New Life Brings A Challenge

Dear Dolly, It's nearly time for Lilli's baby to arrive, so Ron and I started keeping foal watch last week. The weather had been unseasonably warm until the first night that we slept in the tack room. We retrieved our sleeping bags, snuggled into them and waited for signs of a new arrival. Of course it was a little early, but we use any excuse to spend time with the horses at night. I love to listen to the sounds they make. It's such a peaceful feeling.

Over the next several days, I kept Lilli in her paddock where I could observe her closely. I constantly checked for signs of impending labor; by this time, I was fairly skilled at recognizing muscle relaxation, sweating, pawing, colicky behavior and wax on the mare's teats. I saw no signs of foaling until yesterday.

In the morning, I noticed that Lilli was pacing the paddock more than usual. Instead of consuming large quantities of hay, she only inspected it and walked away. Around 3:00 p.m. I brought Lilli into the birthing stall and wrapped her tail. I then noticed wax on her nipples and a little sweat on her shoulders. I fed her and she ate a light meal, but this time she snatched her hay and paced, seeming very uncomfortable and agitated. In the evening, she stood with her backside resting on the stall wall for quite some time. At other times, she shuffled from one side of the stall to the other, glancing at me quite often as I sat on the bench in the hallway.

At 10:00 p.m. we turned the lights out and Ron went to the house to sleep (by this time the excitement of the nightly vigil had worn off). As soon as the barn was dark, Lilli started pacing and urinating. She would grab a bite of hay and walk, then she would stop and stand at the stall door. I watched her in the nightlight from the tack room observation window. She knew I was there, though, and made a point to stop just where I could see her.

By 10:15, I was certain that she was going to foal, so I called Ron to come back to the barn. As he was sneaking back inside, Lilli's water broke and she lay down. She immediately stood back up and I noticed that the foal's feet were out. They were pointed in the right direction, so we both relaxed. When the foal was halfway out, Lilli quickly stood up, I assumed to reposition the foal. As swiftly as she had stood up, Lilli lay down again and this time she quickly pushed the foal out. We fought the urge to go into the stall this time around. We were determined to give Lilli a chance to bond with this foal without our interference.

In the dim light, we could see that the foal was working its way out of the amnion, and Lilli soon reached around and started to assist. Then the foal sat up weakly. We decided to enter the stall at this point. Ron dried the baby and announced that we had a filly. In spite of myself, I had to take a few pictures of the mother and baby. I went about it quietly and I don't think Lilli minded at all.

The foal finally stood and nursed after two hours, and then only with assistance. I thought that this was a little odd, especially since Lilli had gone beyond her expected due date, and also because the filly was very large. But the initial imprinting went well, Lilli had expelled the afterbirth in a short time and was already munching on hay. The filly had passed meconium, moved around a bit and had taken several naps.

Dolly, we're blessed once again with a beautiful foal and a proud mother. Let's doze a little while we're waiting for the vet to arrive for the checkups. 'Night, Dolly

ഇരുഗ്ര

Dear Dolly, The vet arrived very early this morning, examined Lilli and the foal and pronounced them both fit. But a very comical thing happened. Instead of a beautiful filly, it seems that we have a beautiful *colt.* Boy, were we embarrassed! The vet said that he wouldn't charge us a penny for Sex Education 101. Isn't that hilarious?

The vet also said that it was unusual for a colt, especially one this big, to take so long to stand and nurse. He said that colts were usually on their feet with rapid speed, but that he didn't think it was anything to worry about. The vet conducted a test to determine if the foal received adequate antibodies from his mother's milk and the blood's protein level was fine.

I noticed that Lilli was very anxious while we imprinted and when the vet examined her and the baby. In her past pregnancies, Lilli had been very calm throughout and had never minded anyone being near her or the foal. This time, however, she had to be restrained while the vet examined the colt. He told me to keep a close watch on Lilli and let him know if she didn't settle down.

I hope that what's happening with Lilli is normal and not a sign that she's in pain. I brought her a bran mash and she seems calmer now. Think good thoughts. 'Night, Dolly

ෝ෬

Dear Dolly, I'm sorry that I haven't been in touch, but we have had our hands full over the past several days. I know in my heart that you were guarding us, but my therapy will be in telling you the story:

Last Saturday, Lilli and the colt were in the paddock getting some fresh air. As I observed them from the barn, I noticed the colt attempting to nurse several times and stopping. He would just let the milk dribble to the ground. On further observation, I noticed that Lilli had "bagged up" and was streaming milk continuously. I knew that a healthy foal should keep his dam drained at all times. Something was definitely wrong.

I called the vet and explained the situation. His first thought was that the colt had been too greedy and had overindulged on mother's milk; he said that it was not uncommon for colts to do this. He was on his way to another call and said that he would call back within the hour to see how things were going.

In the meantime, I brought Lilli and the colt back into the barn. I then noticed that he had watery, greenish diarrhea. I panicked, knowing that a colt can get dehydrated in rapid time. Without the ability to nurse, it was a dire situation. This baby was in jeopardy, and the hour I waited for the vet to call back seemed like an eternity. When I told the vet that the colt had diarrhea, he said that he was on the way. He told me to blanket the colt while we waited. We hoped for the best, but feared the worst.

When the vet arrived, the colt was standing weakly against the wall of the stall, shifting his feet back and forth. He had a dull look to his eyes, where before he was very alert. Initial examination showed no fever, so the vet gave him an injection of Banamine and started an I.V. to restore fluids to his body.

Lilli was very agitated during the examination and had to be restrained. She seemed easily spooked, which was unlike her. She had always been a calm mother, but we attributed this behavior to her concern for her sick colt.

The vet left with instructions for the night and made arrangements to come out the next day. We kept vigil overnight, on pins and needles every time we went to check on the colt. Our worst nightmare was looming over us. What if this newborn didn't make it?

Early the next morning, the vet came out to find the colt in the same condition. The medicine had stabilized him through the night. We would have to take action immediately if we wanted to save this precious life.

The vet drew blood on both Lilli and the colt; he analyzed it on the premises, which saved valuable time. Nothing irregular was found. Lilli had developed a heavy discharge, and upon examination the vet found that she had a slightly elevated temperature. She was given an antibiotic while he ran another I.V. to the colt. By this time, the colt was not even attempting to nurse, but the liquid diarrhea continued. The vet said that we needed to talk.

He sat down with Ron and me and relayed the options: 1. Take the colt and Lilli to a 24-hour facility, in this case

University of Tennessee; 2. He would make daily trips out to treat the colt; 3. We could learn how to treat the colt and take responsibility for his treatment; or 4. (This was impossible to consider) Put the colt down. We knew that the hospital would be very expensive, although it would be the best bet; the bill for the vet would be insurmountable if he made daily trips out; and letting the colt die was not even an outside option. It might have made sense business-wise, but neither of us have ever made business a higher priority than our hearts. Before we made the decision, however, we talked with the vet at great length about the costs involved for the other three choices. As the vet walked away to give us a moment to speak privately, the colt struggled to his feet and walked over to Lilli and attempted to nurse. Ron looked at me and said, "We have to save him ourselves. I can take time from work and stay at home to help nurse him back to health. If we don't try, I will never be able to live with myself."

So, the decision was made. We listened to the vet as he patiently explained and wrote down exactly what needed to be done. Not only did the colt need round-the-clock care, Lilli had an infection that the vet believed had been passed to the colt in utero. This would explain his weakness at birth, the shivering, and most importantly, his distaste for his mother's milk. I have never seen a more pitiful sight than this baby trying to drink milk and being unable to.

The first thing that the vet did was pass a tube through the colt's nose. Through this tube we were to administer electrolytes every four hours, Foal Lac milk every four hours and Pepto-Bismol every fours, with the times being staggered so that we wouldn't overload his small stomach. We also took his temperature every four hours and he was given hip shots of DMSO and Banamine nightly. In addition, Lilli had to have her temperature monitored every four hours and was milked twice daily. We were novices in equine health care, let alone emergency care. But I have always heard that in a crisis, you do what you have to do. For seventy-two hours straight, we both doctored and kept vigil, sometimes drifting off to sleep just in time for the alarm clock's ring.

126

It was heartbreaking to watch the colt shiver as he did when the cold liquids went into his stomach; on top of this, the weather had turned cold and rainy. To help alleviate the coldness of the foaling stall, Ron installed a heat lamp in each corner.

This morning, we began to notice that the colt appeared to be more bright-eyed, although he still had diarrhea and was not nursing. But after five days of administering continuous medication to the colt, the lack of sleep took its toll on us. We were trying to sneak a nap around noon when I awoke to a loud, unmistakable sound – a nursing slurp! The colt got in two gulps before he walked away. We were so relieved; we knew that this was only a minor achievement and that we had a long way to go, but it was the first positive move the colt had made. At this point, all fatigue left us, and we spent the rest of the day watching as he nursed several times. The number of swallows slowly increased and by tonight he was nursing with almost normal regularity.

I know that we are not out of the woods yet, but I feel encouraged beyond belief. If the colt continues to improve, we will still have to worry about the possibility of stomach ulcers. So much medicine has been pumped into his tiny stomach that it will take some time for him to get well. We will have to keep watching for signs of discomfort for a while. But I'm beginning to feel optimistic about this foal's recovery. We'll sleep a little easier tonight. 'Night, Dolly

෪ඦ

Dear Dolly, Good news! The vet said that we can now stop giving the colt his nightly shots. I'm very happy about that, because it was heartbreaking to hear the colt whine when the needle pierced his skin. With everything he had to go through shortly after his entrance into the world, we have been afraid that the imprinting would fall by the wayside. We wouldn't blame him if he never let a human being touch him again.

The colt appears to be on his way to recovery, and he is now passing "cow pie" manure. He is also munching on hay, which we have kept to a minimum. Lilli is back to normal also and her laid-back manner of mothering has returned.

While he was examining the colt, the vet asked if we had named him yet. I told him that we felt that the colt had to have been touched by an angel, and he was truly a blessing to us. So we named him Gabriel's Blessing, and we call him Gaybe.

The vet removed the stomach tube, a major deal for Gaybe and for us. He also said that he felt guardedly optimistic that Gaybe would be all right. He then gave us a big compliment. He said that a lot of people wouldn't have made the sacrifices we did for a horse, but the fact that Ron and I took on the responsibility says a lot for the kind of people we are. We were face-to-face with the loss of a precious life, but we both can say that we would do it all over again.

Anyway, we are both sleep-deprived, so we are going to take a snooze. Would you do us a favor and watch over Gaybe? Just call if he needs us. 'Night, Dolly

৪০৫৪

When Gaybe was born I didn't notice the warning signs of his condition early on. This is what you should look for:

- ৫ঃ The foal should stand and nurse without assistance within two hours of birth.

- ৫ঃ While it is normal for a foal to take short naps after nursing, increased time down or grogginess is a sign that something is wrong.

- ৫ঃ The foal should pass meconium and not appear to be uncomfortable when urinating or having a bowel movement. The first hint of diarrhea is an immediate red flag.

- ৫ঃ Watch for lameness or swelling in joints. Examine closely for redness or puffiness around the navel stump.

- ৫ঃ If the foal appears interested in nursing but can't, it could mean that he is too weak or something is wrong with the mare's milk.

Chapter Fourteen
Making A Change

Dear Dolly, I don't have to tell you about the week we had. On Wednesday, our farrier was trimming the horses' feet when he mentioned that he needed to find a home for his twenty-two-year-old Quarter Horse. Knowing that Ron had never really gotten over me selling Jerry, I started asking questions. It seems that Showdown had been on the trails most of his life, and he had worked cutting cows and herding cattle. He had been a qualifying horse for Boy Scout merit badges and had taught countless neighborhood children how to ride. The farrier also said that he learned his trade by shoeing Showdown. The farrier called Showdown the king of the trails.

I just jokingly said, "I'll trade you a three-year-old for him." I was referring to Diamahn 'Lil. My reasoning for this was that she was not progressing in the round pen with me, and I felt that the bond we had was too strong. She needed to be ridden and worked every day, and I don't have time to raise babies, ride Whizteria, Maria and Lilli, work Summer and train Gaybe. Surprisingly, he said, "You know, that's not even a trade. You're basically giving away a beautiful Arabian filly. But I'll sure take her and train her. All I want is for Showdown to have a good place to spend his last years." He also said that I was a kind soul to take him in and lose money on Diamahn 'Lil. I told him that while I am in the horse business to make money, it is not my only motivation. I wanted Diamahn 'Lil to have discipline, but more importantly, I wanted her to have someone to work with her and let her live up to her potential.

Diamahn 'Lil gave the farrier a hard time when he tried to trim her feet. She had been good in the past, but now this new problem surfaced. I told him about having a problem getting Diamahn 'Lil to move away from me in the round pen. He asked if he could try her. I was elated and hoped he would prove me right in the theory that Diamahn 'Lil felt so bonded with us that she was in a state of confusion.

I watched as the farrier led Diamahn 'Lil to the round pen and closed the gate. Just as I had expected, she ran from him out of fear. The reason she would not run from me is that she felt that I was her mother figure. Why would you run from your mother? He worked with her for an hour and half, and finally she "joined up" with him. He remarked that she was pretty stubborn. I knew that already, but I was pleased that Diamahn 'Lil could benefit from round pen training.

The farrier and I agreed to do some thinking about the feasibility of the trade. That night, I mentioned it to Ron. At first, he thought I had lost my mind, but then he realized that we would get a seasoned trail horse that could be the teacher for other horses. Ron would also be getting a trusted mount that he could take into the wild, wild west territory of Tennessee. The idea was growing on Ron and I detected a faint sparkle in his eyes.

Last Saturday, we went to the farrier's grandfather's house to meet Showdown. When we arrived, Showdown was letting the neighborhood children ride him. He was very gentle with them, seeming to know that he was carrying precious cargo. I didn't ride because I was suffering from a migraine headache, but Ron immediately liked Showdown and felt comfortable riding him. There was no turning back now, so the deal was made.

The plan was for the farrier, his wife and a friend to bring Showdown and load Diamahn 'Lil. I told the farrier that Diamahn 'Lil had never been loaded, and he immediately said, "It might get ugly, then." "Here we go," I thought to myself, "All of the begging I did to get Ron to help load Diamahn'Lil in the trailer when she was little is coming to fruition." Ron's theory that grown horses will simply load themselves was about to be tested at Diamahn 'Lil's expense. I could smell disaster.

At least we still had the benefit of daylight savings time. The trio arrived around 6:00 p.m., bringing Showdown to his new home and intending to take Diamahn 'Lil to her new home in Bowling Green, Kentucky. Showdown immediately made himself at home in his stall. The farrier decided to work Diamahn 'Lil in the round pen for a little while to get control of her. By the time that was done it was getting dark, and I became increasingly concerned about the outcome of the trailer loading.

The minute she was led to the trailer, Diamahn 'Lil planted her feet and refused to move. She had been my baby, so her reaction to all of this unfamiliar machinery was to look over at me with fear in her eyes. Mind you, Lilli is Diamahn 'Lil's mother, so stubbornness is bred into her. She had absolutely no intention of boarding that bottomless pit.

Repeated attempts were made and every long lead rope we had was broken. The friend tore the ligaments in his shoulder while trying to help and had to go to the emergency room. Through the whole process, I tried to physically remove myself from the area because I knew that Diamahn 'Lil was confused and would cooperate even less if I were around. It really hurt to see her flip over numerous times, and finally when the halter cut into her throatlatch, we had no other choice than to call the vet. By that time it was nearly 9:00 p.m. and the vet was not happy about coming out at that hour. He stitched her up and in a very tactful way told us that she was shocky and didn't need any more stress that night.

The farrier and the vet discussed sedating Diamahn 'Lil the next time they tried to load her, perhaps into an open stock trailer instead of the closed two-horse trailer.

The farrier had told me that his experience loading horses consisted of Showdown (a seasoned performer) and his friends' trail horses. That was a far cry from trying to load a terrified three-year-old that had never been on a trailer. My fears had been realized; and looking at Ron as the vet had stitched his baby up, I saw that he knew that just waiting and hoping the horse would take the appropriate action was terribly irresponsible.

After the vet had finished, we discussed how to proceed. I told the farrier that I would put Diamahn 'Lil in a stall and

131

that they could come back and work with her tomorrow. They left and I cried. I cried for the innocent foal that had been our first, the one that had grown into a beautiful yet stubborn filly. I cried because I knew that the farrier was our best chance to see Diamahn 'Lil off to a new home. But mostly I cried because this disaster was totally avoidable.

That night I slept in the barn to be near Diamahn 'Lil. She stood, wearing a sheet, barely moving through the night, medicated with painkillers and held together by stitches and salve. The next morning Diamahn 'Lil went out in the paddock with her buddies, moving slowly. I spent much of the morning observing her. Ron was visibly shaken and said that all it would have taken was for me to say *stop* for him to call the whole deal off. I replied that the problem would have still existed if he refused to help load her. I was very upset with the whole situation.

The farrier and his wife came back after church on Sunday to begin working with Diamahn 'Lil again, without the trailer this time. I had always gone anywhere in the pasture and Diamahn 'Lil would simply walk up to be haltered. But when she saw the farrier she ran and ran – a heartbreaking game of hide and seek. I turned my back and walked away. He asked me if Diamahn 'Lil was hard to catch, and I told him that she was just playing with him. He knew that the best way to catch a horse is to act like you don't want to. Sure enough, Diamahn 'Lil simply couldn't stand the farrier's 'don't care' attitude. She had to go see what was wrong with him. She stood very quietly and let him halter her without further horseplay.

Diamahn 'Lil had numerous cuts and abrasions that had to be doctored, and I let them do it. I was so accustomed to taking care of Diamahn 'Lil through all of her misfortunes, it was difficult to let someone else do it. But ownership had changed hands and I had to let go. After the appropriate medicine was administered and all the cuts were salved, the farrier proceeded to work with Diamahn 'Lil in the round pen, again attempting to join up. This time it didn't take as long, but she was still apprehensive about him. He didn't attempt to load her this day, but instead he began to fashion a "trailer" by boxing an area in with my cavaletti poles. He had her walk over them and into the box over and over again. He worked with her all afternoon and said that he would be back the next day to take Diamahn 'Lil home. We waited on pins and needles.

The next day, the farrier and his wife came back with a trailer that they had rented from the Co-op. It was more open than the first one and he hoped that Diamahn 'Lil would load easily into it. I asked the farrier if he wanted any help, and he said that he thought they could handle it. I gave his wife the medication and salve that the vet had left. I also gave them a book I had bought called "Trailer Loading Success". The farrier promised that he would read it and teach Diamahn 'Lil to be a trailer loading queen.

Then I hugged Diamahn 'Lil good-bye and told her that I loved her. I hope she knew that I was sorry for the pain she had to endure because we had been irresponsible humans. But I don't think I will ever forget the sad look in Diamahn 'Lil's eyes. I hated to walk away from her, but I knew that I had to. As I turned and started walking away, the farrier asked me if I wanted them to stop by the house to say good-bye. I said no, because it would be too difficult. It would be better this way.

The farrier worked with her for an hour, and she still wouldn't load into the trailer. At this point, it was a matter of will. The vet had left a sedative just in case. I don't know if the farrier used it, but finally they had her on the trailer. They drove away and waved as they left. I would not let myself cry until the farrier's wife called about three hours later and told me that they had unloaded Diamahn'Lil, doctored all her wounds and put her into her new stall. At that point, I lost my composure and cried inconsolably. They promised to keep me informed of Diamahn 'Lil's progress in her new home.

The vet told me that Diamahn 'Lil would probably have no physical scars from her ordeal. I hope that there are no

mental ones, either. However, the farrier thinks she will probably always hate his guts. I appreciate your listening to my frustrations, Dolly. I just need another good cry.
'Night, Dolly

ଛଉଷ

I made a serious mistake by not insisting that we train Diamahn 'Lil to trailer load when she was a foal. Thankfully, she recovered from her injuries, but the results could have been different. Here are some how-to's on trailer loading an older horse:

- ଓ If you have partitions in the trailer, take them out before you attempt to load the horse.

- ଓ Lead the horse to the rear of the trailer and put the lead rope over his neck.

- ଓ Allow the horse to look, sniff and paw the trailer floor, but don't give him the opportunity to back up. If for some reason the horse does back up, reposition him and keep his nose pointed toward the trailer.

- ଓ If no movement has been made after several attempts, tap the horse's hindquarters with a short whip. If the horse takes even the slightest step forward or leans into the trailer, praise him and allow him to rest.

- ଓ When the horse puts one or all feet into the trailer, offer a lot of praise. Sometimes it will take a long time for all four feet to be inside the trailer.

- ଓ To back out of the trailer, fasten a long lead rope to the horse's halter and, standing beside the trailer, put backward pressure on the rope. Allow the horse to back out on his own. Most horses are tentative about the drop off the trailer, so backing the trailer into a low area or ditch to make it as close to ground level as possible will help you be successful.

Dear Dolly, On Sunday, Ron had his first real 'get acquainted' ride on Showdown. For the first time since Jerry left, I saw a real excitement in Ron's eyes. This horse, although twenty-two years old, is in excellent condition and has experienced everything possible on the trail. Now not only would he be Ron's trail buddy, Showdown would be the teacher for horses that are new to the trail.

Showdown was indeed used to being the only horse. When food was around, he would kick at anyone or any horse near. I soon learned to isolate him when I fed him outside. I also make it a point to bring him into the barn last, because he likes to canter in. It is a game to see how I can outsmart him into being the last horse in the barn. Shamefully, Showdown had not had treats before. Imagine a horse living that long without carrots, Dolly. I vowed to change that. Showdown is in remarkably good shape for his age, but to be certain, I asked the vet to check him out. Aside from teeth that needed floating, Showdown proved to be in excellent health.

Then, just two days ago, I noticed that Showdown was lying down in the pasture around 3:00 p.m. This was very unusual, so I started observing him. He would stand up and paw, then lie down immediately afterward. "Uh, oh, signs of colic," I said to Ron. I brought Showdown inside the barn, and once in his stall, he just lay down and made no attempt to get up. I made a call to the vet's office and while I waited for his return call, I thought about how we had so looked forward to having a seasoned trail horse to teach our other horses and to be a trail buddy for Ron. Yes, we knew that Showdown was old and we fully expected him to live out his last days with us, but this was too soon. I prayed that this episode would pass.

The vet called back and said that he would come out and tube Showdown and that we would need to watch him carefully for signs of manure passing. He did this within an hour and Ron slept at the barn that night. About 2:00 a.m. Ron called me through the intercom to say that Showdown had just pooped! We were so excited! Only horse lovers can understand this reaction. Yesterday morning, I withheld grain and fed Showdown only hay. I kept him in the small paddock during the day and observed the passage of manure. He seems back to normal. Thankfully, it looks like we will have Showdown for a while. At least I hope so. I'll let you know how things go, but if you have any influence on the powers that be I would appreciate a little help. 'Night, Dolly

∞∞∞

Dear Dolly, I had forgotten how much fun trail riding can be, but last week I had a chance to get back some of what had been lost around here. We took Showdown and Maria to a park near here and rode the trails. Everything was fine until the weather suddenly turned blustery and cold. We decided to end the ride early and were making our way back to the stable, but we kept getting lost. Then a weird thing happened when Ron turned Showdown to the right. Instantly Showdown planted his feet and wouldn't budge. Maria stood firm, waiting for a cue from her hero. No matter how hard Ron tried to get Showdown to move, he just stood there.

Knowing that this was not characteristic behavior for Showdown, I tried to figure out what was wrong. The only

thing I could think of was that this was not the path Showdown was used to taking when the farrier had ridden him before. I mentioned it to Ron and he said, "Well, he's not led me down the wrong road yet, so I have to believe him." He then turned Showdown around to the left and we made it back to the stable in record time.

When the farrier came out Monday, we mentioned the incident to him. He laughed and told us that the right turn led to an old logging trail that would have taken another hour to complete. Showdown knew that! He sensed the urgency of the weather situation and knew the shortest route back to the stable. Showdown is proving to be a good horse to have around, but I think we need a compass. Graze a little and enjoy. 'Night, Dolly

ଔଔ

Chapter Fifteen
Life Goes On At Summerwind

Dear Dolly, Things have really become slack around here. I've been a little lazy and have barely been able to put one foot in front of the other to do my chores. To make up for lost time, I decided to put Summer in the training mode, and worked her in the round pen for a little while. Summer is going through what I call the "yearling craze". I call it that because each of our babies went a little berserk at that age – nervous, skittish and a little stubborn. What was once sweet and precious now has turned into mule-like tendencies, kind of the terrible two's for horses, I guess. I didn't know anything about handling these babies, Dolly, but I started Summer according to the gospel of John Lyons. She ran around and around without listening and after three minutes I tried to stop her. She just kept running. I let her run for another three minutes and yelled for her to stop. Again she kept running. I tried again and this time when I put my arms up Summer stopped and turned to look at me. I was very impressed. I walked toward her and placed my hand on her forehead. We had "joined up". I'm going to work with Summer three times a week until we get this round pen technique down pat.

I have bent your ear more than once about the problems I had with Diamahn 'Lil. I don't want a repeat of that, so I'm hoping to use my lesson learned from that experience to teach Summer properly. 'Night, Dolly

⁖☙

Dear Dolly, Lunchtime was a hoot today. Ron had just come home for lunch and as I came into the kitchen, I looked out the window out of habit toward the barn. A strange man was closing the gate to the backyard. He then rang our back doorbell. As Ron went to open the door, I said, "Who's that strange horse in the backyard?" Lo and behold, a bay Quarter Horse had made himself right at home in our yard! After introductions, the man explained, "I was coming up the road and got behind him. I figured he was lost, so I followed him. When he got to your driveway, he turned in like he knew where he was going. I just assumed he lived here, so I was putting

138

him up for you." We had a great laugh over that. I said something along the lines of, "I guess he's heard that the best place in the county for a horse to live is Summerwind Farm." That might be true, but the question remained: Who did he belong to?

The man started riding back up the road to see if anyone was searching for a lost horse. Just about that time a neighbor came up to see what was going on. By coincidence, she raises Quarter Horses, but he didn't belong to her. While she was visiting, some more people came up to look, but there were no takers. About an hour later, a truck and trailer driven by a cowboy came up to the barn. As it turns out, the man and his wife had taken the Quarter Horse in on consignment and their stallion had been biting him. I figure the Quarter Horse had taken all he could stand; he jumped the fence and sought refuge with us. At any rate, they loaded the horse and were on their way. He had some pretty serious-looking cuts and bruises, but they called to say that the vet checked him and he should be all right. For a long time to come, I will probably look out my window and fully expect to see that horse in our backyard! I've had enough excitement for one day. 'Night, Dolly

ᏸᎧᎶ

Dear Dolly, We have been working with Gaybe since his illness to retrain imprinting and leading, but I believe now in first impressions. Even with all he went through when he was ill, he remembers it all. The only touchy spot with Gaybe is his hind feet; Ron thinks that the series of shots he gave him in his behind daily had a lasting impact on him, but I think that with time, that too will pass.

Although Gaybe is now beginning to eat hay regularly, he hasn't been touching the sweet feed. I remarked about this to the vet who said that Gaybe probably knew it would hurt his stomach and was wise enough to refuse it. However, after about a month of me offering and him refusing, he has begun to mouth a little. Gradually, I hope to be able to get him started. It has taken a full three months for Gaybe to develop a taste for sweet feed. His mother's milk, on the other hand, is another story. And after his ordeal as a newborn, we are very glad to see him nurse with vigor. Babies are grand, aren't they? 'Night, Dolly

ಐಂ೮ಐ

Dear Dolly, It's been a while since I told you about the horses' antics, but I'm back and ready to share. They were all due for their semi-annual vaccinations early this month, so about a half an hour before the vet arrived, I brought them in and gave them a little of Lilli's alfalfa as a treat. Maria, who is somewhat of a glutton, gobbled hers up quickly. Suddenly, she began choking and streaming greenish-yellow saliva from her nose and mouth. All the veins on her body popped out, and she began to sweat. She looked at me in a panic-stricken way, as though she were asking for help. I tried the best way I knew how to soothe her. I quickly called the vet, who confirmed that he was 10 minutes away. He told me to reassure Maria and to try to calm her, but not to panic because she would be okay. When the vet arrived, he put in a nose tube, and immediately the glob of alfalfa went on down.

The vet instructed me to strip Maria's stall of everything edible and to withhold all feed from her that night. Dolly, you can only imagine the heartbreak I felt at feeding time. Maria would nicker to me and beg with her eyes. Ron slept at the barn to keep watch over Maria and aside from the sound of her munching on the stall door, he said that all was quiet. In the morning, Maria was elated to receive a light meal of grass hay and was very content.

I'm going to be more careful when I choose hay, Dolly. That incident really scared me, not to mention Maria. 'Night, Dolly

ಐಂ೮ಐ

Just when I thought we could relax a little, I now faced another dilemma – in the middle of the night, Whizteria would let herself out of the stall and stand in the hallway of the barn. To make things worse, she chose to stand in front of Maria's stall, thus making Maria very upset. One night, Maria almost kicked the door down. Every evening, I would make sure the latch was secure, only to be awakened by the monitor in the wee hours of the morning. I guess we were lucky that Whizteria didn't feel free to let the others out as well. To

140

solve this problem, Ron lowered the latch so far that even her exquisite Arabian neck could not allow her to reach it. This has not lessened Whizteria's ambition, though. She still tries to open the stall door every night.

Another comical little problem is my bright idea to have a window between two stalls. When we built the addition to the barn, we left the existing front window in place and added a stall next to it. My thinking was that the horses in those stalls would enjoy looking at each (hence socialization) and certainly it would create better air flow in the barn. How could I have known that Whizteria would find a mother idol in Maria? She stood by that window every waking and sleeping moment, much to the chagrin of Maria, who loves her privacy. Each night, Maria made such a commotion that we reluctantly closed the window. Maybe two other horses will occupy those stalls some time in the future and we will have better success with it, but we won't try it with Maria again. Some horses just don't want to be social, do they? 'Night, Dolly

ക്ര

Dear Dolly, Lilli and Gaybe graduated to the big pasture with the other horses and he was easily accepted into the herd. One reason probably was that he is a big colt, almost as big as Summer, who is nine months older. We were amazed at his rapid growth. It was almost as if he had to make up for lost time. My point is that Gaybe is a big, beautiful, strong colt.

I have heard that babies will take up with those closest in age, and it is true of Gaybe and Summer. From the time he was first introduced to Summer, they have been best pals. Summer is his half sister, and between her and Diamahn 'Lil they took care of Gaybe. Diamahn is his full sister and she looks a lot like him. The major marking difference is Gaybe's four white stockings. Diamahn 'Lil was a good baby-sitter and now we look to Summer to take over the job.

I once again began to concentrate on riding Whizteria and Maria. Whizteria had just turned four, and I worked her in the arena instead of the round pen. She pulled the usual spooking – you know, at trees, grass, sticks, anything that moved. Whizteria definitely had an objection to the far end of the arena, and it was always a fight to get her to go forward in that direction. But it occurred to me that I routinely lunged her at one end of the arena only, so I began to work her on the lunge at both ends prior to mounting, and she began to calm down. She is an easy horse on which to post and I continued my practicing.

Maria, on the other hand, seldom spooks, but doesn't lunge well. I use the John Lyons' 'Round Pen Reasoning' method on her. She is extremely good at listening to commands and stops on a dime. Every one of her gaits is good, and she still has a low natural carriage. Her rocking-chair canter is my very favorite, although I have to remind myself that I need to practice everything with her so that she remains this way. Soon we will head for the trails again.

A funny thing happened tonight with Maria. We have accumulated several barn kitties from the animal shelter and they routinely sleep in the stalls with the horses. Tonight, however, Maria obviously didn't want a companion and Nickers, the top cat in the barn, jumped up onto her stall door as she stood waiting for hay. Maria pinned her ears at Nickers, but he stayed there. She pinned her ears at him again and this time she shook her head at him. Still, Nickers stayed put. The third time, Maria picked Nickers up with her teeth and slung him across the hall of the barn. Thankfully, Nickers was not injured, but from that moment on he understood the term "moody mare".

It's bedtime and I'm going to do a last check on the horses. See you in the morning. 'Night, Dolly

ഇന്ദ

Dear Dolly, Gaybe is now four months old, so I have weaned him. Prior to doing this, I asked the vet about his illness and whether it would impact the ability for him to adjust to separation from Lilli. He said that as long as Gaybe had been eating on his own consistently and if he was showing steady weight gain, then he saw no reason not to wean him. I knew it was for the best, as he was really draining Lilli, who was beginning to show signs of weight loss. So, on a bright, clear Sunday morning, I turned Lilli out in the high pasture away from Gaybe. I kept him with Summer in the paddock next to the barn. He did beautifully, except every three hours he would walk the fenceline and call his mother. Once in a while Lilli would respond, but being the seasoned broodmare that she is, she soon fell silent. That night, I put Gaybe into his own stall (he had been having his meals there for a month) and left him. He was a very big boy, and as the stall was next door to Summer's, they touched noses all night. It seems that Summer instinctively knew that Gaybe needed comforting and she delivered, big time.

With the weaning of Gaybe complete, I now started working Lilli again. She went from bad to worse. I had not ridden her since the autumn, but I think even if I had worked her every day she would have taken an attitude with me. Lilli was constantly behind the bit, and she would put her mouth on the ground and trot, even when I cued her to walk. I began to think about Lilli's bit and wonder if I needed to change it. Shelby had used a Tom Thumb bit with Lilli and so far it had worked well, but I thought maybe I needed to try Lilli in a snaffle bit. I had read that snaffle bits are the mildest ones and that a horse can be re-trained easily in them. It was worth a try.

Lilli was impossible to handle with a snaffle bit. I couldn't get her to stop at all. She ran around and around the arena and I let her run. When I could control her enough to get her to slow down to a walk, I could stop her fairly easily. But when I put Lilli into a trot again, she took off and wouldn't stop. After several scary attempts, I changed my mind and figured Shelby must have used the Tom Thumb bit for a reason.

I spoke with Shelby about this. She has never particularly cared for Lilli and thinks she expects royal attention. It is true that Lilli is a prima donna, but she does have a history of abuse. I think I tried to overcompensate for that by making excuses for her behavior. Maybe I love her too much. Get some heavenly rest. 'Night, Dolly ৩০০৪

Dear Dolly, Gaybe is six months old and is starting to demonstrate that he is a little stud by pushing and shoving a little. He is also beginning to develop biting tendencies. I stopped that by putting a nail in my hand with the point sticking out between my thumb and forefinger. When I entered his stall and he came at me biting, I let the nail bite him first. I never showed aggressive signs myself, but rather, I let Gaybe bump into the nail. Within three days, all attempts at biting stopped and they have not resurfaced.

There was never a thought in my mind that Gaybe would be a stallion, so I wanted him castrated. I had heard that the sooner it is done, the better. I made an appointment with the vet. He said that he would check to see if the testicles had dropped and if so, he confirmed that it would be better to do the procedure now than when he was older.

On the day of the appointment, all checked out well. The vet anesthetized Gaybe, who immediately went down. The vet asked Ron to put a towel over Gaybe's face and kneel on his neck in case he tried to rise during the surgery. The procedure went as scheduled and the testicles were removed in their entirety. Gaybe was out cold for about thirty minutes, and then with a snap he sat up and started to get to his feet. Within ten minutes of surgery, he was walking in the stall. The recovery went very rapidly and without incident. We really appreciated an uncomplicated event for a change.

Things seem normal right now, Dolly and I am so happy about that. It seems that we have had a lot of challenges to overcome. A little bit of dull would be good for us.
'Night, Dolly

ഇരുരു

Chapter Sixteen
An Agonizing Decision

Dear Dolly, Part of my therapy has been to visit Shelby and her husband at least once a year to work with my own horses, but this year I decided to leave everybody at home and just assume she would have a horse that I could ride. Boy, did she ever have a horse! I went to North Carolina at the end of October and had the best time! First, Shelby had been caring for a Paintabian yearling colt that had developed stomach ulcers while with another trainer. He had lost weight rapidly and had spent two weeks at NC State School of Veterinary Medicine. Shelby then decided against all advice to take him on and try to restore his self-esteem and physical health. Second, she was training the leading two-year-old dressage Warmblood in the United States, which had suffered some kind of puncture wound in the chest the week before. The mare was swollen all over and felt very much like bubble wrap when touched. She was the funniest sight, but the vet said that she was not in pain, so I had the privilege of riding her.

This mare is a cross between Shelby's Arabian stallion and a Percheron. At two years of age, she is already over 16 hands tall. When I rode her, it felt like sitting in an easy chair, but she could really move. This is the horse I really learned to post on. I hadn't planned it that way, but all of a sudden I heard Shelby say, "Up, Up, Up"! That young man once said that a light would just come on in my head. Well, the light beamed and it all worked out beautifully. I hope to ride her again, and each time I call Shelby I'm going to ask if Lo is still there so I can plan my next visit.

Then I woke up one morning and said to Shelby, "I'm going to ride Pete today." Now, Pete is Shelby's husband's prize mule and not just anybody gets the honor of riding him. I opted to do it without him knowing. Of course, Shelby thought I was crazy, but she went to the pasture with a very large halter and brought Pete to the barn for what I'm sure he thought was a big meal. Then she placed an orange plaid jumper saddle pad on him (that was funny enough) and an English saddle and bridle. Pete's head is very long, but the bridle that he wore fit him perfectly. Then we proceeded to the arena, where I made an attempt at lunging Pete. Talk about funny! We laughed so hard at the way I stood in the middle of the arena with Pete sporadically taking off and stopping around me. Finally, it was time to mount.

While Shelby stood by, laughing uncontrollably, I used the mounting block (which I don't think Pete had ever seen before) to get on. When I applied pressure with my legs, Pete stood still. When I applied more pressure, Pete stood still. When I kicked lightly, Pete stood still. When I kicked really hard, Pete took off like a lightning bolt. I slowed him to a trot and actually posted! It was short, choppy posting, but as Shelby said, if you can post on Pete, you can post on anything.

Shelby snapped lots of pictures of Pete and me to remember the occasion. But the funniest part of the story is when I re-told the event to her husband, who could not believe that I rode Pete. He said, "Now, Emily, you know I don't let just anybody ride Pete." But he said this with a twinkle in his eye, so I knew that all was well. I must say that even though riding Lo was very special, the highlight of my trip was posting on Pete!

I'm really glad to be back home at Summerwind. Did you take care of all the horses for me? I wasn't worried at all with you watching over us. 'Night, Dolly

ജന്മ

Dear Dolly, I came back from North Carolina all boosted up and eager to put my experiences to good use. Although I was riding Maria and Whizteria in the arena, I really wanted to get Lilli back on the trail again. I remembered the good times we had before Lilli developed her kicking habit. Maybe Lilli would have a different perspective if I could get her out into the world again. Could it be that she was simply bored with riding in the arena?

I decided that I would start riding Lilli on our property and gradually work up to the trails next door. The first time she was ridden in the front yard, she was great. The next time she acted a little weird, but I survived; and the next (and final) time the ride started out fine. Lilli and I followed along behind Ron and Showdown to the creek. When I attempted to cross with Lilli, she refused. Even though I knew that it was a mistake to let her get away with it, I decided not to try and cross. My safety was foremost in my mind at that time, and given Lilli's behavior over the last year, I know I made the right decision.

I started to walk her back and forth across the yard, rather than making a straight line toward the house and barn. Suddenly, Lilli started bucking and spinning. When I got her stopped, she immediately started backing up and spinning. For the first time in my life, I was truly frightened on the back of a horse. This horse that I had made my own, who had been my salvation from a life of stress, was now a major source of stress. I called out for Ron and said, "This is it. No more." He offered to ride her back to the barn. I thanked him, but said that I had to do it. Lilli was perfectly happy to be going back to the barn, so I had no problem with her from that point on.

When we got back to the barn, however, Ron suggested that we not let her get away with it. He asked me to ride Showdown back down to the front yard and he offered to follow on Lilli. That really ticked me off, because here was a man who had never been around horses until I forced them on him. *I* taught *him* how to ride, and now he was suggesting that he ride Lilli when I had problems with her. How dare he? Well, I needn't have concerned myself, because the minute Ron mounted Lilli, she proceeded to back him up into the side of the barn. He bailed right off.

With a cloud hanging over me, I called Shelby yesterday and told her that I thought I should sell Lilli, because any horse that didn't appreciate a nice home with a room and maid service didn't need to live with me. Shelby said that in her opinion Lilli would best be advertised as a broodmare, because she is an excellent mother and is a beautiful, exotic-looking Arabian. Although I am not actively pushing the sale, if the right situation comes along, I will part with Lilli. I know that I bought her too hastily and for all the wrong reasons. However, I did everything I could to care for Lilli and to try to erase the abuse that she had suffered in the past. Maybe I over-compensated and let Lilli get away with bad behavior. Dolly, I love Lilli with all my heart, but I know that I won't try to ride her again.

When I think of all I went through when I first bought Lilli and all the problems I encountered with her, it really pains me to give up. But a horse that has no regard for my safety scares me, and fear is not the reason I want horses. Instead of the freedom from stress I longed for with Lilli, all I have is more stress. My heart is heavy with this decision, but I think it's time. 'Night, Dolly

ཀ୦୦ଓ

Dear Dolly, With the trailer-loading disaster with Diamahn 'Lil so fresh in our minds, Ron saw the error of his ways and suggested that we start teaching Summer and Gaybe to load.

Gaybe, who suffers from no fear, loaded twice right away and backed out on his own. We thought we had it made. Then it was Summer's turn; she had no intention of going into that black hole. Summer stood and pawed at the floor, but after about two hours we had made no progress. Then I had the bright idea of backing the trailer into the arena, where all she had to do was step straight into it. *Not!* After this method and constant tapping on her upper hindquarters didn't work, Ron decided to try a butt rope.

B. Shield ec1

Summer panicked as soon as the butt rope touched her rear, and all 94 pounds of me had to let go of the lead rope. Summer run like a bat out of hell, dragging the lead rope along with her. She finally ran into the barn, where she threw herself against the back gate. The gate bears the brunt of the damage and is bent where she hit it several times. Summer didn't escape without lots of scars to add to her inventory. She also didn't load that day and typical of us, we let the trailer lesson fall by the wayside. We both know that Summer had won that battle, but the war was indeed not over yet.

The next crisis occurred during the farrier's visit. He said that he had ridden Diamahn 'Lil and that some girls at the stable were thinking about showing her. He added that all her scars had completely healed, except perhaps for the emotional ones. Diamahn 'Lil now loads very well and it seems that she is on the right track, training-wise. I'm happy that she has a good home now.

On this particular day, Gaybe decided that he was a big boy now and didn't need his feet trimmed any more. When the farrier started to pick his feet up, Gaybe folded and leaned into the farrier. He did this over and over again, until the farrier said, "Let's lay him down." The farrier, his wife, Ron and I all proceeded to the round pen. Do you have any prediction about the results? Gaybe did not lie down at any time. I think that this bloodline of Lilli's, regardless of how regal it is, has a streak of stubbornness a mile long. After an hour of struggling, I asked him to quit. I didn't want a repeat of what happened to Diamahn 'Lil.

Dolly, that brings you up to speed on the happenings around here. Go to sleep in green pastures under the stars.
'Night, Dolly

৪০৫৪

Dear Dolly, I think this is the best season of the year for horse lovers and as Christmas is approaching, we have started to decorate the barn. We can only hang decorations there, because of the menagerie we have in the house: four cats, a golden retriever named Meggan and Molly, herd-dog extraordinaire. Anything that goes up in the house comes down immediately or is chewed beyond recognition.

I had an idea to design a stocking for each horse with its name on it, which were then stapled outside the stalls out of reach. We also strung horse Christmas lights up on the rafters and put wreaths on the front doors of the barn.

One evening, I went to the barn as usual, and as I was giving the horses their hay, Ron asked, "Where's Whizteria's stocking?" On further examination, we found it on the floor of her stall, with the toe eaten out. Leave it to that long,

Arabian neck; Whizteria had stretched and stretched until she got a hold of the stocking and down it came. This time when we put it up, it was a good five feet away. I dared her to touch it again!

Two days before Christmas, Ron and I went to the local animal shelter to make our yearly supply donation. I peeked into the cat room while Ron unloaded the truck; in a moment I heard him call, "Emily!" I ignored him. "Emily! You have to come into the dog room." "No," I said. "We already have two dogs and four cats!" Still, Ron pleaded. "Okay," I said, "but I will just look, and then we're leaving". I followed him back to the dog room where my eyes fell on a mixed breed dog of questionable origin. The dog looked at me as if he knew I came there just to see him. He looks like the dog from the old television show *My Three Sons*.

Raggs makes his home with us now. Molly and Meggan welcomed him with open paws, and he is a very sweet, if ugly, dog. We keep hoping Raggs will look better, but we think he is a reincarnation of an ugly dog we had years ago. Anyway, Raggs is Ron's Christmas present.

Dolly, I hope you had a great Christmas in the heavenly skies. Ours was good because nobody was injured or sick. I hope you had a lot of extra clover. 'Night, Dolly

ഇൻരൂ

Dear Dolly, A lady I know from the feed supply store mentioned to me last week that she was going to Colorado to ski and needed someone to care for her horse, a ten-year-old Quarter Horse mare named Hannah. An idea began to form in my head and I asked if she was good on the trail. The lady said that she had been ridden all over Tennessee and had never spooked. I suggested that the mare stay with me while she was gone. It sounded like a perfect solution. The mare would be well taken care of and I would get to ride her on the trails.

On Saturday, Rita and her husband brought Hannah to her new home away from home. She backed off the trailer with no problem and followed Ron to her new stall. All of the other horses called out to greet Hannah as she made her way down the aisle of the barn. I felt very proud of myself for having such a wonderful idea.

Yesterday, Ron and I saddled Showdown and Hannah and went for a long ride. Hannah was perfect and didn't spook once. Showdown was on automatic pilot and behaved admirably, as well. I brought Hannah back to the arena and rode her to see how she behaved in that environment. She listened to me as I put her into a trot, then a canter. But when I cued her to stop, she kept cantering.

I let Hannah canter around the arena one more time and asked her to slow to a walk. Then I asked her to canter again. This time when I asked her to stop, she listened to me.
That was the only problem we had.

So, Dolly, I think the first ride went well. In hindsight, maybe I should have worked Hannah in the arena before I went on the trail. What do you think? Next time I'll do it the other way. 'Night, Dolly

కుండ

Dear Dolly, Today I put my training to good use by taking Hannah to the arena before Ron and I went trail riding. She was as good as gold and listened to my every cue. Then we hit the road.

Ron and Showdown were a good twenty feet behind us. Hannah was walking along with not a care in the world when all of a sudden two deer ran out in front of her. Dolly, she bolted with lightning speed. Thank goodness I had learned from my experience when that hornet stung Maria a few years ago. I talked to Hannah quietly and eased her down to a slow canter, then a walk. She slowed willingly and I was relieved that I was still sitting on her back.

I'm glad the rest of the ride went smoothly. I would never have survived in the Wild West! 'Night, Dolly

కుండ

Dear Dolly, I know I'm beginning to sound like an old record, but it's been a while since you heard anything from me. I know you witnessed the whole thing, but I need to vent, please.

Last Saturday was Hannah's final day with me, since Rita was coming to pick her up on Sunday morning, so I decided that I wanted one last ride. Over the two weeks that Hannah was at Summerwind, she had exhibited some signs that made me a little anxious. For example, she was extremely quiet when we were on the trails in the woods, but when we came to a clearing or she caught sight of the barn, Hannah immediately started picking up the pace. I didn't think too much of it, though, because I had no trouble bringing her back to a walk.

The worst habit I had detected in Showdown was his desire to graze while we were on the trail. But because we wanted to make sure that Showdown's last years were special, Ron and I both indulged him. Before he came to live with us, he had been allowed to graze at different points on a trail ride. Showdown was so easy to control that we didn't see a reason not to continue letting him pick at grass. Besides, our grass was dead with winter and the meadows that we passed on our trail rides were lush with green grass.

Hannah had evidently been given the same privilege, because she kept trying to put her head down to graze even when we didn't give the go-ahead. But there again, she was also easy to pull up and move forward.

We were turning toward home from our ride when Hannah gave me the first indication that trouble was brewing. The minute she spotted our barn, Hannah moved into a trot. I brought her back to a walk and circled around behind Showdown. For a little while she walked along beside Showdown and then she speeded up again. This went on for the rest of the ride and I breathed a sigh of relief when we crossed the culvert and were back in our front yard again.

Hannah and I were about thirty feet ahead of Ron and Showdown. I made the decision to canter Hannah crossways across the yard while I was waiting for them to catch up to us. When I cued Hannah to slow to a walk, she put her head down to graze and caught me completely off guard.

I grabbed the reins to move her forward, but then Hannah took off in a gallop. This time I couldn't get control of the reins and she had her freedom. I was caught off balance and tried to regain my seat, but each time I recovered, Hannah jerked me in the opposite direction. I kept calling for her to walk, but it just got worse.

All Ron could do was watch as I was jostled all over Hannah's back. Then my feet came out of the stirrups and I knew I was going to be airborne.

I tried to think of the best way to land, but in a split second there isn't enough time to make an intelligent decision. So I told Ron that I was coming off – and then I did.

Dolly, the end result is that I broke my collarbone, had three crushed ribs and a collapsed lung. I also had my first ambulance ride and a six-day "vacation" in the hospital. While I was recuperating, I replayed the fall over and over in my mind. I wished a million times that I had done things differently, but it all happens so fast that common sense goes out the window, along with rider training.

I know you've seen Ron at the barn doing chores. He has really had a busy schedule. Before he goes to work in the morning at his regular job, he has been feeding, cleaning the stalls and grooming the horses. Then at night when he comes home he feeds them again and spends time with them at the barn. That's all in addition to taking care of me. What a great guy he is! And a tired one, I'm sure.

Hannah went home the day after my accident. Rita was very upset when she learned that I had been injured, but I look at it this way: Horses aren't computers and even the best horses can have bad days.

When people ask me about the accident, the inevitable question is, "Are you going to ride again?" And my answer is, "Of course." I can't imagine not riding. I've heard that the best way to learn to stay on a horse is to fall off a horse. That couldn't be truer. Accidents happen and I'm not about to quit riding.

It will be a while before I'm back to doing barn chores. Right now I'm thinking ahead to the spring and being able to get Maria on the trails again. That gets me by for now!
'Night, Dolly

಄಄

Since my accident, I have heard several people say that their horse grabs grass when they ride on the trail. I know from experience what a dangerous habit this can be. Here are some thoughts:

- ಅ Stay alert to your horse's moves and be consistent in your discipline. Don't let the horse have grass one day and expect him to walk on without trying to graze the next.

- ಅ Use your legs to keep the horse moving forward when you anticipate that he is going to stop or snatch grass at the walk.

- ಅ Avoid pulling on the reins to jerk the horse up. In my situation, I did this and it resulted in Hannah being stronger than I was. I became unbalanced in my seat and she won the battle.

Dear Dolly, The past few months haven't been much fun for me. I was gradually able to help Ron with the barn chores, but the physical therapy really drained my energy. Too, I lost my taste for food or any kind of drink and had to force myself to eat. But slowly and surely, I made strides toward recovery.

One Sunday I decided that I had had enough of being idle. Ron had ridden the trails with Showdown all winter long. He's the one who got to fasten sleigh bells on Showdown's saddle and ride in the snow. I was very envious of that, because we had planned to take that ride together. It was to be the ride that brought back the memories I had of you pulling the sleigh in the snow when I was a child.

I had watched Ron ride away on Showdown too many times and I decided that I wasn't going to wait any longer to get back on a horse. I wasn't wearing a brace now and I felt that my ribs had healed enough for me to ride. While Ron and Showdown were gone, I waited patiently in the tack room and practiced my delivery.

When Ron returned home, I met him at the gate and told him that I was going to ride, if only for a short distance. He urged me to wait, saying that he didn't think I was ready yet. Naturally, I saw this as his way of over-protecting me and not allowing me to make my own decisions. Emphatically, I once again insisted that I was going to ride. Ron knew that I had made up my mind and agreed. I asked him to hold the saddle while I mounted.

I had forgotten one very important thing: I couldn't lift my arm high enough to grab the saddle. The left arm worked fine, but the right arm wouldn't cooperate. Each time I tried to lift my arm, the pain was unbearable. I even tried to mount with the aid of a mounting block, but this was not successful, either. You know how I hate to give up, Dolly, but I had to this time. I went back to the house feeling dejected and depressed.

I think that healing works in different degrees. The degree I have reached now tells me that I need to bide my time and work harder in physical therapy. Believe me, I'm really going to concentrate on my recuperation. I have to get back in the saddle – and soon. 'Night, Dolly

ജ‍ൽ

Dear Dolly, Spring is approaching and my thoughts are turning to the breeding season. I'll tell you more about that later, but first let me share my riding experience. It was the best therapy.

You've been there as a sounding board for me during these last few months and I thank you. You've listened to me cry because I was injured. You've heard me say a million times, "I wish I had been more alert." You've been silent when I complained because I couldn't ride yet. Well, Dolly, today is your lucky day! You don't have to hear my complaints anymore, because today I rode Showdown!

I've been trying really hard to build strength in my upper arms and it paid off for me. Ron held the saddle as I mounted and for the first time I was able to lift my arm high enough to get on. Showdown was very gentle, because I think he sensed that he had a very nervous rider aboard. And, Dolly, I *was* anxious about riding. It's funny how all my self-confidence on horses just evaporated when I was injured.

We had a good ride around the front yard and Ron watched me from a distance, making certain that he didn't seem obvious. When I rode back and halted Showdown at the front of the barn, Ron said I had a giant grin on my face for the first time since I fell. I could feel the tension leave my body after that ride. I can't describe the feeling, Dolly, but I get it every time I ride a horse. There is nothing in the world like it.

Hopefully, things can return to as normal a pace as we can expect around Summerwind. I can now look forward to planning for next year's babies. Thanks for putting up with me.
'Night, Dolly

ಸಿಆ

Chapter Seventeen
The Breeding Season And A Place In Time

Dear Dolly, I want to share the happenings around here with you. Shelby had mentioned that she thought Maria would have a beautiful foal if she were bred to a black and white Paint stallion. I thought this was a great idea and began to search for one. Shelby had intended to help me, but her father had recently been diagnosed with a serious illness, so her energy was needed there.

I picked up an Arabian magazine and began searching for the right stud. We had also been given a computer for Christmas and I used it to search the Internet. After several days of searching, I found a horse farm that had a homozygous, EE black and white Paint stallion that was really beautiful. I know that terminology means nothing to you, but it means that the foal is guaranteed to be black and white in color. The farm is located in eastern North Carolina, and they advertise that they will ship semen. That would be perfect for our situation. After what happened to Shaikh, I didn't want to send Maria seven hundred miles from home to be bred. I contacted the owner and, satisfied with her answers to my questions, I sent her the booking fee.

You know that my dream has always been to have two babies to run and play together, but the timing has not been right – until this year. Whizteria is almost five years old now and is ready to breed. Her bloodlines are among those that have produced many halter champions, and I had already decided that I wanted a gray foal. As luck would have it, I remembered a couple who had visited us at Summerwind last year. The man had mentioned that they had a three-year-old stallion that they would be standing for the first time this season. He is a steel gray grandson of Bey Shah, one of the leading sires of Arabian halter horses. It sounded like a win-win situation, so I called the breeder and asked for pictures and pedigree information. I was very pleased with the match and happily paid the booking fee that same week.

With the commitments for breeding in place, I started tracking estrous cycles; Maria is a very demonstrative mare who exhibits coming in season by lots of talk and kicking out. On the other hand, Whizteria is only four years old and shows few signs of estrus. I asked the vet to check both mares to make certain that everything was in order reproduction-wise. Maria checked out fine, and her culture was negative. Since we will be doing artificial insemination and Maria won't be traveling, the vet said that a Coggins test would not be necessary.

Whizteria already had a negative Coggins, but he said that her reproductive tract is small and that the breeder would need to use a breeding roll; that is simply a stick covered with a towel that is placed over the rectum area so that the stallion cannot penetrate the vagina too deeply. I called the breeder and she said that they were familiar with the procedure, although they had not needed to do it before. We started considering artificial insemination for that reason, but we did not make the final decision. I would be reluctant to use artificial insemination when the breeder lives thirty miles away, but the horse's safety is always foremost.

With that said, I'll let you take a nap now. I have much more to tell you later. 'Night, Dolly

୨୦୯୫

Dear Dolly, While we were waiting for the horses to cooperate with the spring breeding season, we decided to work on trailer loading. Since the weather was beginning to warm up, we felt that we were ready to brave the elements. Given the history of my having to fight Ron to get him to hitch the trailer and help me try to load, a positive sign that he was willing to help meant "move forward while he is in the mood".

Maria was a seasoned traveler, although she had not been trailered since the year she went to Shelby's in North Carolina for breeding. Whizteria had been shipped many times, but the last occasion was her trip to her new home with us. And it goes without saying that we had two babies that needed to have trailer- loading lessons.

I am still very tentative with my injuries and was not very helpful at all during our attempt to load the horses. All I could do was give direction and offer moral support. Maria was loaded first into the trailer that Ron had backed into a ditch, making the step up very small. However, our tried and true Whizteria balked and backed out as soon as she saw Maria in the stall beside her. That wasn't good thinking on my part; Whizteria is intimidated by Maria and should not have been loaded after her. Ron backed Maria out and started trying to load Whizteria by herself. Some two hours later, only her front feet had made it into the trailer. I decided to quit, even though I knew she had won. I commented to Ron that this incident proved the importance of consistency in loading horses and he fumed.

We then tried to load both Gaybe and Summer, with the same hesitation on both parts. I asked Ron to dig out a space in the arena where the trailer could be backed to ground level. He did this and chocked the wheels on the trailer. Then I put Whizteria's evening meal in the trailer. At first, she didn't understand what was required of her. After a half-hour of running around the arena, Whizteria figured out that if she wanted to eat, she needed to get with the program. She stepped onto the trailer and ate with no problem. The next morning I did the same thing, taking Whizteria out of her stall and to the arena for her meal. A week of doing this turned Whizteria into an enthusiastic loader. She no longer balks at the trailer and does not need food to climb on board.

We used this technique only once with Gaybe, who as a yearling was so curious he couldn't stand it. He just had to try everything. He jumped into the trailer, making all kinds of noise, turned himself around and walked back off. The next time he let Ron back him off the trailer. It was then that I really saw our efforts in teaching young foals to move forward and back on command pay off for us.

Summer also loaded fairly well, but she was slightly leery after her incident with the butt rope, so we are taking our time. After all, unless the world ends, Summer is going absolutely nowhere in the future. We will just teach her how to trailer load, because it makes a good foundation, not because she is going to be sold. Besides, who knows when one of the horses will become ill and have to go to an emergency hospital? What will we do if we can't get them loaded?

Well, Dolly, as you can see, we have our hands full with these horses. It's nothing at all like life with you. You never rode in a trailer, as far as I knew. In fact, most of the horses that I knew growing up were transported in the back of a pickup truck. I believe you walked everywhere you went, didn't you? 'Night, Dolly

ൟ

Dear Dolly, You are really sensitive to my thoughts, so I know you feel my excitement for this breeding season. Anxious to get things rolling, I called the vet to come out and check Maria. My intention had been to breed and confirm pregnancy on Whizteria first, but since she showed no signs of coming into season, I decided to concentrate on Maria first and then breed Whizteria a month later. The vet thought that was a good idea, because it would also give Whizteria more time for her cycles to get stronger with the longer daylight hours.

I had started to chart Maria's cycles, and as nearly as I could tell, she was close to ovulation. When the vet checked her, he decided that he would give her a shot of prostaglandin to aid in the process and make the ovulation easier to pinpoint. This way she should come into season around Friday, and hopefully ovulate by Sunday. I called the lady who would be shipping the semen and relayed the information to her. She said that she would be going to a horse show for the weekend and asked if the vet could check Maria on Friday instead. That way, she would collect and ship the semen before she left for the show. If not, she would not be back until Sunday afternoon, and the earliest we could receive the semen would be Monday.

I called the vet, and he indicated that he still wanted to wait until Saturday with the hope that Maria would not ovulate before Monday, but he said that he wanted the semen here as early as possible on Monday a.m. After several e-mails back and forth, it was decided that the breeder would collect the

161

semen when she returned from the show on Sunday afternoon, then air freight it for an arrival in Nashville at 11:30 p.m. Ron joked about his midnight run for semen, and prayed that the highway patrol wouldn't stop him. How would he ever explain that? I told him that a true horseman would tell the patrolman that he was going to the airport to get semen. Thank goodness he wasn't stopped by the highway patrol, because I'm not sure Ron is that much of a horseman yet.

He was home by 12:30 a.m. Monday and the vet inseminated Maria around 11:00 a.m. He said that the timing could not have been better. The second insemination was on Tuesday at 7:30 a.m. So now we wait for the sixteen-day ultrasound and keep our fingers crossed. You, too! 'Night, Dolly

ଈଓଷ

Dear Dolly, You can see from the look on my face that Maria is not in foal. The good news is that the vet said that she has two equal-sized follicles that would be ready in two days. I scampered to e-mail the breeder to ask for another semen shipment. Plans were made for Sunday (which, by the way, is Maria's birthday) and we were to call the vet when the semen was in.

He also checked Whizteria and found no follicle, so he asked me if I wanted him to give her a shot of prostaglandin. I told him to go ahead. She reacted extremely well, and I went to call the breeder. We had made the decision, after talking with the vet and the breeder, to go ahead with natural breeding. We completely trust this breeder and feel that Whizteria will be safe in her care. The vet said that Whizteria should be taken to the breeder's barn by the weekend to settle in, so the breeder came to pick her up on Saturday night. Hopefully, she will be ready to breed for the first time by mid-week and be back home by the weekend. I really miss her and each time I walk by her stall, it seems too clean and too quiet. She is always the first one to call me when I open the back door each morning. Strange how you get used to that! 'Night, Dolly

ଈଓଷ

Dear Dolly, We've had more challenges with Maria. On Sunday morning, the breeder e-mailed me to explain that she had collected the semen and was on her way to the airport, with the shipment arriving in Nashville at 3:00 p.m. I called the vet and advised him of the time frame. He said that his new associate would be on call, and I was a little nervous about that until the vet assured me that he had watched him inseminate mares all day long. He said he felt really comfortable with him and that I should, too.

By 3:15 p.m., Ron had picked up the shipment and I had paged the vet. He said that he would be here at 4:00 p.m. He was right on time and did the first insemination. Maria still carried both follicles and since they were still small, he inserted an Ovuplant, a hormone stimulator, under the skin of her neck. This implant would make it easier to pinpoint the exact time of ovulation. My understanding is that sperm can live inside a mare for up to seventy-two hours, so the timing was good. The vet came back on Monday at 4:00 p.m. to do the second insemination. I wish for the best, but I won't get my hopes up this time. Maria's sixteen-day ultrasound was scheduled and all we can do now is wait for that day to come. 'Night, Dolly

ဆဝင

Dear Dolly, Whizteria was bred on Wednesday, Thursday, Friday and Saturday. The breeder said that she behaved like a seasoned mare. She joked that Whizteria kept calling for the stallion afterward and he was so exhausted that he hid behind his feeder. It was really funny to hear her relay the story of these two sweethearts. The breeder's husband brought Whizteria back on Saturday night and said that he almost didn't bring her home because he loved having her there so much. They are very excited about the possibility of a baby between these two beautiful gray horses.

Whizteria's sixteen-day ultrasound found her to be in foal. We were ecstatic and called the other grandparents right away. The thirty-day ultrasound was also positive and we breathed collective sighs of relief. Dolly, I am so thrilled to have Whizteria in foal. I still think back to how she would stand at the fence for hours at a time watching Summer when she was a baby. Now she will have her own baby to watch. I just hope that Maria will cooperate and I can realize my dream of two babies to grow up together. Think good thoughts. 'Night, Dolly

৪০৬৪

Dear Dolly, Ron and I discussed at great lengths the wisdom of artificial insemination. The security of having Maria with us for the duration was definitely a plus. But as far as the expense goes, I wouldn't do it again with Maria. First of all, there is the problem of multiple ovulations; secondly, the costs of each shipment, plus additional vet fees for each insemination, are not cheap. We had set aside a certain amount of money for this effort, and we had calculated that we could try three times. If Maria's ultrasound didn't turn out positive, we would have to call it quits.

Words can't tell you how disappointed I am. My dream will not become reality this breeding season. Maria is not in foal, and in addition to exhausting all our funds the season is over for the breeder. She has asked me to consider sending Maria to her barn next year. Although it is a long haul, I'm fairly sure that we will do it.

On the other hand, we are so looking forward to Whizteria's baby and can't wait for that day to come. Naturally, we are concerned for Whizteria's health, since this will be her first foal. But we feel blessed to be able to anticipate the birth with her. But, Dolly if you thought I was a worry-wart with Lilli and Maria, just imagine how I will be when Whizteria is due. You might want to take a vacation from here and fly somewhere peaceful while all of that is going on.

I believe that everything happens for a reason and that something positive comes from the experience. Maybe the good in this situation is the fact that Maria and I can get back on the trail this fall. We will look ahead to next year's breeding season . . . and dream. Your childhood friend is both happy and sad. 'Night, Dolly

৪০৬৪

Dear Dolly, This morning, in an instant, the United States of America changed forever. I spent the morning in the barn as

164

usual, grooming the horses and mucking stalls. I left the dogs in the basement, because the feed store was making a delivery and I didn't want them to be in the way. The deliveryman had called and said that he would be out around 10:00 a.m. but as the morning turned to early afternoon, I began to wonder if he had been in an accident. I thought several times about going back to the house to check my phone messages, but I didn't want to get the dogs upset. I continued to wait for the deliveryman and focused on cleaning the tack room.

The truck finally pulled in at 1:30 p.m. The driver got out and apologized for being late. He asked me if I had been watching television. I said that I hadn't been in the house since early morning. I asked why. He told me.

At first I thought he was joking, but I couldn't imagine anyone joking about airplanes crashing into the twin towers of the World Trade Center, the Pentagon and another crashing in a remote field in Pennsylvania. The devastated look on the man's face told me that he was serious, and my heart sank.

How could this be? What kind of madness causes a catastrophe such as this? I knew that there would never be an acceptable answer. So many lives had been interrupted and the pain their families and friends would suffer was unimaginable.

It seemed like the deliveryman unloaded the feed in slow motion and as soon as he was gone I turned and ran to the pasture as fast as my legs would carry me. Once there, I went from horse to horse, hugging each one and crying. I cried for the lives lost and the shattering of our nation's innocence, but I also cried selfishly because I was still here. You were always sensitive to my feelings, Dolly, and today I realized that all horses must know when their human is sad. Under normal circumstances, each one of those horses would have pulled away from me in a short span of time. But today all of them, including Showdown, let me stand with my arms wrapped around them while I sobbed.

I can't explain my next move, but it seemed like the right thing to do. I put a lead rope around Maria's neck and led her to the paddock. I saddled her, put the bridle on and took her out to the front of the barn. She waited patiently for me to mount and then we rode down the side of the yard toward the creek. I asked Maria to cross the creek and then we headed for the trail.

Dolly, that was the best ride I've had in a long time. Maria and I were in complete sync today. You know, there's an old Winston Churchill quote that says, "The best thing for the inside of a man is the outside of a horse." That trail ride with Maria on September 11th was the best thing that I could imagine for me.

Like most Americans, I spent the next few days glued to the television, captivated by the events that unfolded and inspired by the heroes of that day. It made me grateful to be an American and I will make a conscious effort to live each day to the fullest.

Watch over our world as you go to graze and pray for our future. You're a kind soul and I'm glad you're here.
'Night, Dolly

ഔ൫

166

A Final Word

Dear Dolly, When I think of everything Ron and I have been through over the last five years, I am very proud of our progress. I spoke before about Ron's lack of experience with horses, but I was truly a novice when I started riding again. You spoiled me for any other horse because you were such an easy keeper. When I decided that I was going to spend the rest of my life caring for horses, I had absolutely no idea what I was doing. I think the word novice was invented for me in this instance.

I will have to admit that my dream of living with horses was deflated a little when I realized that there was considerable expense involved. But where there is a will, there is a way; I have worked diligently to cut operating costs and am constantly looking for new ways to be thrifty.

Has it been worth it? You bet! Regardless of the trials and pitfalls of our first five years, I believe that Ron and I were meant to be together at Summerwind Farm. To be honest, the road between us has been rocky at times. But one thing is for sure: the reasons for staying with this endeavor far outweigh throwing in the towel when things go wrong. We have made a dream into reality. We have a long way to go in our horse-keeping venture, but isn't that what a dream really is?

A dream is realized when you know what you want and you make it happen. That's exactly what we're doing. I'm living a dream come true and it all started when I re-discovered you, Dolly. You gave me the courage to move forward. Because of your inspiration I can wake each morning to the sound of horses in the barn and hear their whinnies when I walk out the door on my way to feed them. I know you're up there watching over us and that you'll be along for the ride as we embark on all our adventures.

Life is good at Summerwind Farm!